£14.95

BLACK DAYS

John Matheson

Hodder Moa Beckett

To my mother, sisters and brothers who will probably never read this book but who will tell me they liked it anyway, and to my dad who will read every chapter, laugh at the fun parts and spend hours contemplating the serious ones.

To Warren Adler and Kevin Chapman at Hodder Moa Beckett for their continued support. To Tim Connell and Andrew Stevenson – if it wasn't for them giving me a chance at *NZ Rugby World*, I would never have had the opportunity to pen this book. And, of course, to all the All Blacks – past and present – who have contributed to the remarkable club that will continue to dominate world rugby well into this new millennium.

ISBN 1-86958-764-2

© 1999 – Original text John Matheson
The moral rights of the author have been asserted

© 1999 Design and format – Hodder Moa Beckett Publishers Limited

Published in 1999 by Hodder Moa Beckett Publishers Limited,
[a member of the Hodder Headline Group]
4 Whetu Place, Mairangi Bay, Auckland, New Zealand

Produced and designed by Hodder Moa Beckett Publishers Ltd

Film by Microdot, Auckland
Printed by South China Printing Co, Hong Kong

Contents

Foreword

Maybe somewhere else in this world rugby is merely a game. In New Zealand we have made it into something much more powerful. We only need to look back to 1998 to know that when the All Blacks are struggling, New Zealand can be a rather gloomy place or back to 1996 when a party atmosphere intoxicated all of us as Sean Fitzpatrick led his side to New Zealand's first series win on South African soil.

We celebrate the All Blacks as soon as we are old enough to hold on to a rugby ball. Most of us celebrate them because of the stories our fathers, uncles and grandfathers tell us about the men who preceded our own heroes.

Every New Zealand male grows up dreaming of playing for the All Blacks. We fantasise about what it would be like to pull on the black jersey... what it would be like to do the haka... what it would be like to score the winning try in an All Black test against the Springboks.

We know about the legends of men like Dave Gallaher, George Nepia, Wilson Whineray, Brian Lochore, Colin Meads, Graham Mourie, Buck Shelford and the irrepressible Sean Fitzpatrick.

But we have heard only one side of the story.

Black Days' purpose is tell tales of the All Blacks from the perspective of the men who had to face up to them.

Men like Willie John McBride, who sent Lansdowne Road into a shivering silence when in his first test against the All Blacks he threw a right hook in the direction of the great Colin Meads... "If I'd known about the legend of Colin Meads I would have thought twice about aggravating him." Men like Gareth Edwards, who grew up believing the All Blacks were giant men who never felt pain... "I remember looking at him and thinking Good God, they do bleed!"

In the course of interviewing twelve of the world's biggest rugby names for *Black Days*, it became clear that the respect for the All Blacks around the world is as strong now in the professional era as it was in 1965 when Dawie de Villiers captained South Africa on its tour to New Zealand.

New Zealanders have a habit of knocking the All Blacks when things on the field go wrong. We are quick to criticise and often treat the players with contempt. The advent of professionalism may make some of us believe that we have more of a right to criticise the modern day player – after all, in a sense we are paying their wages.

It is therefore a sad irony that some All Blacks may feel more respected when they step away from these shores.

Every player approached to take part in this project was quick to add his support to it. The great Argentine first five-eighth Hugo Porta even put his responsibilities as the Minister of Sport in Argentina on hold for his *Black Days* interview.

This is as much a celebration of some of the greatest players to front up to the All Blacks as it is a tribute to the on-going New Zealand institution that is the All Blacks.

John Matheson
Auckland, 1999

Serge Blanco

Date of birth: 31-1-1958
Born at: Caracas, Venezuela
Position: Wing/Fullback
Test matches: 93

"My favourite French back was the wing Serge Blanco who sometimes had the heart of a butterfly, yet under pressure was capable of unleashing an attack which could result in a try at the other end of the field"

Graham Mourie
(**Graham Mourie, Captain,** 1982)

SOMETIMES Serge Blanco talks to the gods. This is not exactly a news flash to some rugby people, that sizable number who would probably tell you it means Blanco has finally found what he considers a peer group. But no, Blanco isn't claiming any special relationships. He's merely describing those nights after a game when he would stay up into the wee hours, sipping a red wine and thinking deep thoughts about how, despite all his planning, so much still comes down to fate.

In the past Blanco has made some other-worldly pronouncements – such as that all the deceased rugby players and coaches are looking down at games and indulging their whims, allowing a last-minute penalty kick to fly through the centre of the uprights or crash into the posts and bounce back into the field of play, or causing a referee to blow a call with the game on the line. So his invoking the gods for his own purposes might sound characteristically off-the-wall. But maybe an occasional chat with the deities is healthy for a player of Blanco's nature. Maybe they remind him that there's only so much a man can control and that the best place to start is with himself.

It was during Blanco's first tour to New Zealand – as a 21-year-old in 1979 – that the lesson was first learned. There was no doubting Blanco's talent. He was carving a niche for himself as one of Europe's most exciting rugby prospects. He was fast and elusive but he was in rugby for himself. "Doing it for the team" was not something he'd grasped at that early stage. But when he returned to France after watching the French recover from a 23-9 defeat at Lancaster Park to record a famous 24-19 victory at Eden Park, Blanco had grasped the team ethic. It was the key to the All Blacks' years of success and it took a tour where he remained in the stands as a spectator to click.

"When you don't play, when you are not even a substitute, a tour answers no purpose. Hopefully, I was young and carefree. It was going on not so badly. Then, this test match had to happen, on the glorious July the 14th, where the French had won for the first time against their prestigious opponent in New Zealand. That was my first contact with victory against New Zealand, and that's all it took to teach me one of life's great lessons. I was so sad to only see from the stands this triumph in which I was not taking part. I would be a big liar if I were saying the contrary. Who can pretend to be proud of watching a team winning without playing? I was happy for them but I didn't jump for joy. How can a player wish happiness to another player when he is not playing himself? This is the hypocritical diplomacy of all players in the world. I even cried when I went in the changing room. Those were the first but also the last tears I have had against the Blacks.

"At home this victory was celebrated as a national event. It was an unexpected success against the best team of the last 50 years. We didn't realise then that – as the 1994 French team taught us – it was possible to do much better. It was possible not only to draw a series against the All Blacks but it was possible to beat them.

"But this day of July 1979 helped me a lot. The French captain, Jean-Pierre Rives, had to set the record straight with me the night following the match. He made it quite clear to me that a player's time in rugby is much too short to feel sorry for yourself. He told me I had to make a decision to be the best player that I could be. I had to make a commitment to French rugby. I had to decide to play for the team – as the All Blacks had done for many years. After that conversation, I understood. Rugby was as much for the team as the individual. It was time to grow up."

Being a part of the touring team to New Zealand that year was not the pilgrimage for Blanco that it was for so many of his teammates. Blanco didn't grow up believing in the myth of All Black rugby. The likes of Wilson Whineray or Colin Meads weren't his heroes. "I mostly admired the Welsh," says Blanco. "Players like Gareth Edwards and Phil Bennett and the others guys with long hair and side whiskers. That's my myth. They were the players I wanted to be."

But once in New Zealand for the eight-match tour, Blanco became hooked on New Zealand rugby. As the team travelled around the country he marvelled at the support the provincial teams and the All Blacks generated. It was the same passion for rugby that he had but instead of it being a personal experience, he was surrounded by the same obsession.

"In New Zealand everybody is concerned with rugby, so much more than in France or anywhere else in the world. In France the rugby roots grow in the south-west. Even though the entire country supports the French team on test day, in New Zealand the roots are everywhere. Strong and proud. In Auckland, Otago, Canterbury – from the north, down to the south. It doesn't matter where you are. Rugby *is* life in New Zealand.

"You can see that in the way they respect the silver fern. I think that wearing it must have a concrete influence on the players. To wear that jersey gives them strength, responsibilities, and an unfailing morale. All of a sudden, they are people who enter the service of their nation. That is probably the biggest difference between New Zealand rugby and all the other rugby of the world.

Each country has its own legend, but in New Zealand the All Black team come before any individual. When you have a look at those two islands on a map, what this little country represents geographically, this is a miracle. The quality of their pool of players is exceptional because everybody is consumed by the black jersey. Everyone is dedicated to the All Black cause. For it, you will give your last bit of energy."

&

THE year was 1987 and France had defeated Australia to win a place in the inaugural Rugby World Cup final. Their opponents would be New Zealand and the venue Auckland's Eden Park. It could have been, perhaps should have been, the greatest day in Blanco's career. His exuberant play from fullback throughout the tournament had cemented his place as one of rugby's great entertainers and his match-up with his All Black counter-part John Gallagher was anticipated with relish.

The game was an anti-climax. The great confrontations – neither Blanco v Gallagher nor France v New Zealand – did not eventuate. The All Blacks dominated the game, with tries from Michael Jones, John Kirwan and David Kirk sealing a 29-9 victory.

While the New Zealand team of the day were in a class of their own – the 20 point margin in the final was the closest any team got to the All Blacks during the tournament – Blanco is convinced his team were beaten long before they stepped onto the field.

"We approached the final in the worst way," he says. "We had lost it even before we played. Before the tournament we were all very upset not to be recognised as one of the favourites to win. We had won the Grand Slam and Five Nations championship a few months earlier but still no one gave us a chance. People were only speaking of New Zealand and Australia. It was as though no other team had a chance. To us, it seemed as though there was a complete lack of respect for European rugby so we entered the World Cup with the intense desire to demonstrate that all those forecasts were wrong.

"During the first part of the World Cup, we were more or less comfortable. We slowly started with a tense 20-20 result against Scotland. Then we played basketball against Romania [55-12] and

Zimbabwe [70-12]. Phew! We'd finished first in our group; we absolutely wanted to avoid the All Blacks in the quarter-finals.

"Because we felt like there was no respect for us we focused totally on making the semifinal. That was our goal. And when we earned the right to play against Australia it was as though we were painting our masterpiece. That day, the unforgettable 13th of June, 1987, in Sydney, we proved that we were a great team. Our true value was clearly shown to everyone. At the very end of the game, we'd succeeded in beating the Australians, with a try in the corner of the field, that I had the luck to score. I think it was already the 85th minute of the game. It was a fabulous joy. But after that game it was as if we had already reached the goal we had planned. Our objective was not to be world champions, but only to thwart the forecasts. This is, above all, the reason why we lost the World Cup. Of course, the All Black team was a great one. They deserved to win. But we were in no state of mind to play against such a supreme team.

"We had always been a team that were concerned with sentiments, with good fellowship, with happiness, with enjoying life. Just before the final, a couple of hours before, we had great discussions born out of an exceptional sincerity. They had no longer something to do with rugby but about a kind of love between us. There was an exceptional respect for each other. It was magic! We said exactly what was to be said. We were happy, proud. That is the reason why that group will never die.

"But as we began to realise what we were close to achieving we got nervous. The more nervous we became the weaker we got. By the time kick-off came, we'd spent too much energy."

The French held the All Blacks to a 9-0 score line in the first half and after Didier Camberabero had landed an early penalty in the second half truly believed victory was possible when they forced three defensive All Black scrums. Kirk then blew the game apart with his try.

"We had the All Black scrum right where we wanted them. But the All Blacks kept collapsing the scrum so we couldn't advance. The last one was only five metres from their line. We deserved to be awarded a penalty try... but this memory, of course, only remains in the French mind. The truth is the only thing people will remember of that day is that the New Zealand team became the first champions of the world.

"And that's fair enough because their win was deserved. New Zealanders have a great talent; they know how to write their destiny. And they also, at the same time, dictate their opponent's destiny. During the final we went through stages when we'd make mistakes – miss tackles, miss kicks, drop passes. That was when the All Blacks would go up a gear. They would take advantage of every mistake and soon our morale was low. The final score was a crushing blow. In the changing room, everybody felt empty. What? Did we really play? We had this funny feeling that those 80 minutes only lasted two minutes.

"But there is no need to curse teams like that All Black one. The best thing is to thank them. They gave a lot to rugby. The Blacks were a very clever group. Their captain, David Kirk, was very good, not only in terms of managing on the field but also in terms of strategy. He was very sensible, very interesting.

"With him were a lot of exceptional players, especially one, John Kirwan, that the world of rugby has probably too quickly forgotten. Lots of things are said about Jonah Lomu and Tana Umaga but, much earlier before them, Kirwan was a phenomenon. I had never seen such a strong winger before, with this mix of strength and speed. Then, there were some very special guys, some players with a unique talent. I am thinking of Grant Fox. This man has not been evaluated rightly. They made him exclusively a striker, with a magic foot, whereas he was a man who was feeling the whole game, who was only making perfect passes, where and when it was to be. More than that, he knew with the foot or the hand how to create massive pressure upon his opponents. He was the one who ensured continuity in the All Black game.

"It would be offensive not to speak about everybody. We could, for example, easily write a book about Sean Fitzpatrick. What about Michael Jones? This guy was incredible. During the nine years when I played against the Blacks, I cannot remember a so complete team as the one of 1987. Both technically and physically they were just so far ahead of their time."

Jones was one of five players on hand in 1987 who were missing from the All Black line-up in 1986 when France had upset the All Blacks 16-3 in Nantes. It's a tribute to the replacement players – Gallagher for Kieran Crowley, Warwick Taylor for Arthur Stone, Fox for Frano Botica, Jones for Jock Hobbs and Alan Whetton for Mike Brewer – that they could be so comprehensive in victory when only eight months earlier they had been completely outplayed by the Tricolores.

For Blanco the test at La Beaujoire Stadium would be the only time he would be on the winning test team against the All Blacks. He'd experienced a victory against the New Zealanders when he played on the wing for a French Barbarians team as a 17-year-old against Graham Mourie's 1977 tourists, but this win was for real. This time he was in the famous blue French jersey playing alongside 14 men who, like him, were men possessed.

French pride had been dented the previous weekend when, despite having the superior scrum, they lost a hard-fought test to the All Blacks 19-7 in Toulouse.

Says Blanco: "When we played them seven days later we knew we had to play the All Black way to win. We had to show a real aggressiveness in the way we would play. We had to be a little bit more manly than we were used to. And we won 16-3 because we were filled with hate because of how we'd lost the week before. We had felt we had deserved to win in Toulouse but the All Blacks played a very clever game. They disrupted our scrum by slowing the engagement down. They never let us dominate the scrum. If they weren't happy with the set, John Drake, Sean Fitzpatrick or Steve McDowell would just stand up. Just like that! Maybe they knew the referee was on their side? We were very disappointed not to win.

"In between the tests we would watch videos of the Toulouse match every day.

"Our coach, Jacques Fouroux, stressed the importance of us recovering our pride in Nantes. He told us that, in order to reach greatness, you have to suffer losses. You needed to know what defeat was like before you could understand the real joy of winning.

"Anyone who was at the La Beaujoire Stadium that day would have known straight away that this French team were not going to lose. I still have this vision of the most intense haka I have ever seen in my career of playing the All Blacks. Eric Champ, our flanker, went and stood in front of Wayne Shelford when he was leading the haka. He had been the first one to do that. We all stood behind him showing solidarity. Earlier in the week someone had told us the haka was a war dance. We decided that we were not going to let ourselves be intimidated by them."

Fouroux's tactics that day were very un-French. The team were instructed to tone down their attacking flair. Victory, not entertainment, was the order of the day. "The tactic was simple," says Blanco. "We decided to put a gun on their head. We wanted to attack them, without letting them breathe even for a second."

It worked. The French held the All Blacks to a solitary Crowley penalty at halftime then, through Denis Charvet and Lorieux, scored two second-half tries to secure only their fifth win against New Zealand.

"It was an unbelievable feeling to beat the Blacks. Unbelievable. I honestly think that our victory could have had more significance and been much more painful for the All Blacks if we'd just played a little better. But when you beat the All Blacks, winning is enough. Against other teams sometimes you want to win well. You want to play unbelievably and score spectacular tries. Against the All Blacks you just want to win. And that day we played like All Blacks.

"Their strength is to always have a well-established team that allows individuals to flourish. Until that year, the French had always believed that the best thing was first to select the men, and then the group would create a culture by itself. That's the Latin way. It sometimes worked. But for the All Blacks, that was something unchanging. For them it is a matter of culture. What keeps their eternal strength is to constantly respect the group's values without ever thinking of the individual value of the players.

"Even today, now that rugby is more destructive than constructive, the All Blacks have found a way to succeed. That way is simply to continue to do what they have always done... play as a team. It is a very rare thing to witness an All Black team needing to rely on an individual to win a game.

"In France, when nothing works, everyone tries alone to save the country. The only time I have seen New Zealand do that was when they lost the World Cup final to South Africa in the 1995 tournament. It was like watching the French! It was as though they were expecting more from individuals in the group than they were expecting from the team as a whole. In was very un-New Zealand-like. Maybe Laurie Mains' tactics were linked to the presence of Jonah Lomu or Josh Kronfeld, exceptional players, beautiful individuals. But for me, Lomu has to give a little more to his team. He should not be the focus, otherwise it becomes a classic French mistake of putting the individual before the team.

"The reason why we beat the All Blacks in Nantes was because of the lessons we'd learned from playing against them. The main one was *give before taking*. It was something the All Black culture seemed to thrive on.

"And this is true in everything: in love, at work, everywhere. When you give with pleasure, you are sure to be rewarded. In a team, with a woman, in every case that life offers, give first and then you will receive. If tomorrow you become selfish, your life is over. That is valid in the whole world. Against the Blacks, we knew that if we were not showing solidarity, we would not be able to do it. Their philosophy of playing was revolutionary for us. On that day, we had done to them what they had done to everyone else. It was a sweet victory."

❧

SOME moments of a career are unforgettable. Others you just want to forget. For Blanco, the latter is a defeat at Lancaster Park in 1986 that still has a high embarrassment factor. For this proud rugby player, it was the worst day of a glittering career.

It wasn't the defeat that hurt... it was who they lost to – the Baby Blacks, an All Black team robbed of their stars who were serving a ban for their part in a rebel tour to South Africa earlier in the year. In all, 12 regular All Blacks were missing – the front row of Andy Dalton, Gary Knight and John Ashworth, locks Gary Whetton and Murray Pierce, loose forwards Jock Hobbs, Mark Shaw and Murray Mexted, first-five Wayne Smith, second-five Warwick Taylor, winger Craig Green and fullback Kieran Crowley. Of the XV that wore the black jersey in the test, only David Kirk and John Kirwan could claim to be first-choice players. While a number of the Baby Blacks would use the test to launch impressive All Black careers – Sean Fitzpatrick, Mike Brewer, Joe Stanley and Terry Wright included – there was no way the full-strength French would lose this battle.

"How could we lose?" asks Blanco. "We were playing second-rate players. Players none of us had heard of. They were like babies. It was, of course, going to be a victory for France."

Blanco's memories of the day are, of course, haunting. The game was lost 18-9, thanks largely to an inspired All Black team and some woeful kicking from Jean-Patrick Lescarboura and Blanco.

"By the end of the game I had been more impressed by our stupidity than by the team we were playing against," says Blanco. "The Baby Blacks played well, that's for sure. They starved us of the ball early in the game and frustrated us for the rest of it. But the performance from Lescarboura and me on that bloody day was unbelievably bad.

"It was a sad day for France – the only consolation now is to look back and see what some of those new players became. Men like Sean Fitzpatrick and Frano Botica had great careers in rugby and league respectively. Now, there is no shame in losing that test... at least that's what I tell people!"

There have been other heartbreaking losses. In Blanco's debut test against the All Blacks in Toulouse in 1981 the French played well enough to win but with All Black fullback Allan Hewson kicking two penalties and a dropped goal the New Zealanders escaped with a 13-9 win. And there was the occasion in 1984, at Lancaster Park, when the All Blacks recorded a 10-9 win after Lescarboura missed four dropped goal attempts in the last six minutes of the game.

"I still can't believe we lost that test," says Blanco. "We dominated the game. Even the referee was against us. Pierre Berbizier charged down a kick and Laurent Rodriguez scored. But the referee, Winston Jones, robbed us of the victory. He was a Welshman who didn't like the French. It is scandalous that this man was able to take victory away. He had already done the same thing to us against Scotland in a Five Nations game. One of our players had nearly been beheaded during a lineout, but he didn't award a penalty. He was responsible for us failing to win the Grand

Slam. And now he was doing the same thing again. But I also know if we had been more skilful with our kicks we would have forgotten about Mr Jones' performance."

In the series' second test, in Auckland a week later, the French were full of confidence. After all, if Lescarboura had managed to land one of his four late attempts at goal France would have been celebrating a memorable victory. But even though both sides would score three tries, the All Blacks, with Hewson landing two conversions and five penalties, would cruise to a 31-18 win.

"It is not just by chance that the All Blacks seem to win all the tight tests," says Blanco. "Having a good goalkicker in the All Blacks is an integral part of the game's culture. For us, this was only of secondary importance. The Blacks have always had great scorers. Bob Scott, Don Clarke, Hewson, Grant Fox. Even today with players like Andrew Mehrtens, Tony Brown and Carlos Spencer they have a huge amount of possibilities. In France we've never had a lot of good specialist kickers. It's a weakness in our game. We seem to always want to play the 'French way'. We attack, we play open running rugby but against the All Blacks it's a risky way to play because you run the danger of leaving an open door on defence.

"Too many times French teams have been naive against the Blacks. We were absolutely naive in the two tests we played against them in France in 1990. We tried to run everything and the All Blacks won 24-3 in Nantes and 30-12 in Paris. We found out many times that more than any other team in rugby, they punish your mistakes. That's why when you beat them, you want to get off the field as soon as possible before the referee decides to give Hewson or Fox another chance to kick a penalty!

"The All Blacks, every All Black team through history, have the ability to give the impression that you will be able to win but which finally doesn't let you do so. It's like you are following them but you never catch them. There are no defeats that don't hurt. You think to yourself: *We are not so far away from them.* But even though sometimes you lose, you can also be filled with joy. Like the game in 1989 at Lancaster Park. They led by 18-0 but we came back to close the score to 18-17. But then with three minutes to go Alan Whetton scored a try and victory was theirs. It is in those circumstances when you feel you've taken on the master. Like the father does to his son, you let the son get close to you, but at the end, you win. Those sorts of games allow you to find a real spirit. Because you are playing against the best, sometimes it's okay to lose, as long as you are learning with every defeat."

❧

REGARDLESS of where you are in the world the reputation of the All Blacks precedes them. They are generally talked about as the best. Master craftsmen, if you like. There have been superstars of the game hailing from places like Wales, Scotland, Ireland, England, South Africa, France, Australia and even Argentina, but for some reason it's the All Blacks that dominate any conversation about greatness in rugby.

Depending on who you ask, the reasons for this are varied. Some mention the pride every New Zealander has in the black jersey. They put it down to the intimidating history that men like George Nepia, Colin Meads, Wilson Whineray, Brian Lochore and Sean Fitzpatrick have helped create for the All Blacks of today. But others – the ones who find it unbearable to pay credit to the All Black ethos – prefer to put the All Blacks' domination down to a nasty streak. Different media around the globe like to portray the All Blacks as ungracious giants. Men who will do *anything* to win. Fitzpatrick at his prime was simply called a cheat. More recently Josh Kronfeld and Jeff Wilson have been tarnished with a similiar label.

"I have heard this talk and it disappoints me," says Blanco. "It is too easy for people jealous of the All Blacks' success in rugby to look for reasons other than greatness for their success. I have always had a lot of respect for the black jersey because when I looked into the All Blacks' eyes I could see they respected me. They respect anyone who is willing to give something for their jersey. In games against them I have been walked on and cut by them. But always according to the rules.

"I cannot respect the English as I respect the Blacks because when I have played against England they have kicked me deliberately, jumped on me with both feet... sometimes it was like they were trying to kill me. This is no exaggeration. Against New Zealand this sort of thing never happened. I was never in fear of the All Blacks. Of course, they always played to win but I cannot say they ever disgraced themselves. It's because when they play they know they are representing the whole magic of rugby. To play against them is the most exciting. Against them, you have pleasure, even when losing, because the New Zealanders have always honoured rugby.

"I am convinced the French have more in common with New Zealand than we have with our European brothers. I know if I went to New Zealand today I would be welcomed wherever I went. And I can tell all the All Blacks that they would be welcomed with open arms if they came to France. Whoever he is. He can call me, he'll have a place to stay, food, and somewhere to sleep.

"This is one of rugby's virtues that helps to bring ferocious opponents together. In order to do so, the after-match was a very respectable institution. Unfortunately, now it is in danger of disappearing. The after-match – in France we call it the third half – was the thing that separated rugby from so many other sports because there were no more winners or losers during those times. It was just friendships; friendships where respect was built."

It was obvious the respect Blanco has for All Black rugby was mutual when he made his last appearance in New Zealand in the second test at Eden Park in 1989. It was the day he won his record 70th cap for France and as a sign of admiration for their teammate the French allowed Blanco to run out onto the field ahead of captain Pierre Berbizier. As Blanco appeared on Eden Park, Berbizier stopped his teammates from following as 38,000 New Zealanders rose to salute the Black Prince.

"They had made me go first and when I turned around I was on my own. The crowd was giving me a standing ovation. A sudden shiver ran through me. This New Zealand public was showing an extraordinary respect, all the more for a player who was not wearing the silver fern on his jersey.

"It was one of the great moments of my career. It hit me in

the heart. I was not feeling the pride because of winning my 70th cap. I was proud because I was alone in this arena and the most knowledgeable rugby people in the world seemed to appreciate me."

SERGE BLANCO AGAINST THE ALL BLACKS

Date	For	Venue	Result	Score	Points
7-11-81	French Barbarians	Bayonne	lost	18-28	
14-11-81	France	Toulouse	lost	9-13	
21-11-81	France	Paris	lost	6-18	pen
16-6-84	France	Christchurch	lost	9-10	try
23-6-84	France	Auckland	lost	18-31	
28-6-86	France	Christchurch	lost	9-18	
8-11-86	France	Toulouse	lost	7-19	
15-11-86	France	Nantes	won	16-3	
20-6-87	France	Auckland	lost	9-29	
17-6-89	France	Christchurch	lost	17-25	2 tries
1-7-89	France	Auckland	lost	20-34	4 pens
3-11-90	France	Nantes	lost	3-24	
10-11-90	France	Paris	lost	12-30	

TEST MATCH CAREER

	P	W	L	D	T	C	P	Dg	Pts
vs All Blacks	12	1	11	-	3	-	5	-	27
All Tests	93	51	39	3	38	6	21	2	233

David Campese

Date of birth: 21-10-1962
Born at: Queanbeyan, Australia
Position: Wing/Fullback
Test matches: 101

"The [1995] series gave me the opportunity to face David Campese. I'd played him in sevens... but it was an ambition of mine to meet him in test rugby. It was important to me to be able to say I'd marked him. Nothing to do with who was boss or anything. He's just been such a great player"

Jonah Lomu
(Jonah Lomu, 1997)

WITH the honours in the first two tests being shared between the All Blacks and the Wallabies, everything hinged on this showdown at Eden Park.

Australia, on the verge of their first series win on New Zealand soil for more than 30 years, were full of confidence after levelling the series with a 19-16 win at Athletic Park two weeks earlier. Within 50 seconds of the kick-off the Bledisloe Cup looked destined to return to Australia. Wallaby fullback Roger Gould had received a pass from Peter Grigg and scored a try which silenced the crowd and sent the All Black coach into a prolonged slump in his seat. After he dusted himself off and landed the conversion to give Australia a 6-0 lead, Gould headed back towards his team.

"What a start," says David Campese. "There we were, six-nil up after less than a minute. It was the sort of start you dream of. The All Blacks were under enormous pressure from the public to hang on to the Bledisloe but it looked like we were gonna snatch it from them. When Roger headed back towards the team everyone was thrilled. There were lots of 'Good-on-ya-mates' but Roger didn't seem to be exactly thrilled about it."

Gould, while lining up his conversion, had been privy to the All Blacks' reaction to conceding such an early try. The New Zealand captain, Graham Mourie – by no means a ranting and raving kind of captain – was laying down the law to his troops. Hardened All Blacks like Murray Mexted and Mark Shaw stood silent, their eyes locked on Gould and their minds focused on immediate revenge.

As Gould accepted the congratulations from his teammates there were no smiles. *I don't know if scoring was very good fellas... you should see how pissed off they look!*

&

IT didn't take David Campese long to make an impression on every New Zealand rugby fan during his first Wallaby tour in 1982. After his selection to make his debut in the first test in Christchurch, local pressmen asked him for his thoughts on his opposite number – All Black winger Stu Wilson. *Stu who?* was his reply.

It didn't matter to Campese that Wilson was well on the way to become the All Blacks' leading try-scorer at the time. And it didn't matter that Campese's throwaway line had put him in the firing line of the New Zealand public for the first time.

"Some people thought I was being arrogant," says Campese. "They probably looked at me and saw a 19-year-old kid who thought he was a lot better than he was. But the truth is I wasn't trying to be smart or arrogant. I just didn't know anything about Stu Wilson. I didn't know much about the All Blacks. I certainly didn't have much of an appreciation for the traditions of the All Blacks. At that stage I just figured that they were like any bunch of blokes playing rugby."

Campese could be forgiven for his naivete. He didn't hail from the private school systems of New South Wales or Queensland. Campese was from Queanbeyan – a small town near the border of New South Wales and the Australian Capital Territory. Every

Saturday morning he'd turn out for the local rugby team and on Sundays he'd switch jerseys and play rugby league. His heroes were typical for a boy from Queanbeyan. His father and older brother filled the void city kids would satisfy with men like Russell Fairfax or Ray Price.

That the legend of David Campese was to be born on the 1982 Australian tour was a surprise as much to Campese as it was to the rest of the Australian rugby fraternity. Coach Bob Dwyer was forced to look for reinforcements for the three-test tour to New Zealand following a mass walkout of Wallaby stars after the 2-0 series win against Scotland just weeks before the start of the New Zealand tour. Nine players – Stan Pilecki, Tony D'Arcy, Bill Ross, Peter McLean, Tony Shaw, Mark Loane, Michael O'Connor, Brendan Moon and Paul McLean – announced their unavailability, citing a lack of time outside rugby to earn a significant income as the reason for abandonment... although to this day there are many who believe it was a sign of support for former Wallaby coach Bob Templeton, who had been dumped in favour of Dwyer.

Regardless of the reasons, O'Connor, Hawker and Moon's unavailability meant Dwyer was looking for a winger. Campese got the call. He made his debut in the tour win against Manawatu and played against Hawke's Bay a week later before Dwyer handed him his first cap. This would be the beginning of a test career that would take in a world record 101 tests and see him score 64 test tries, also a world record.

Campese was one of six new caps in the Australian side which fronted up against Graham Mourie's All Blacks in Christchurch. And while the All Blacks would triumph 23-16 – with Murray Mexted, Steven Pokere, Bernie Fraser and Mourie all scoring tries – it was the 19-year-old from Queanbeyan who stole the show. With his first touch of the ball he introduced himself to Wilson by running around him and in the 78th minute of the test he gathered a Mark Ella cross-kick to touch down for the first time at international level.

"I had no fear that day," says Campese. "If I knew then what I know now, I would have been a bundle of nerves because the more you play the All Blacks the more respect you have for them. But in

1982 I was just a kid. When you're 19 you don't think anything can stop you. You certainly don't think anyone can hurt you. I was more nervous about lining up alongside my idols in the Australian team than I was about playing against the All Blacks. But once that game started... well, it didn't take long to appreciate the All Blacks. I remember seeing the New Zealand guys in their black jerseys and thinking: *Holy shit, they're big bastards!* I realised pretty quickly that test match rugby was like nothing I had experienced before.

"It's difficult to explain what it is like to play the All Blacks. I don't think you can fully appreciate it unless you have done it. It was tough stuff. Every time you got hit, it hurt. Every time you make a mistake you have this horrible feeling that they are going to capitalise on it and make you feel like shit.

"Was it daunting? Absolutely. There is something special about the All Blacks. I ended up playing them 29 times in my career but perhaps the biggest lesson I learned from them came in that first game. I knew then that if I was ever going to be on a side that beat the All Blacks, I'd have to be on a team that played something close to perfect rugby."

While Campese's performance at Lancaster Park was eye-catching, it certainly wasn't perfect. There were a couple of dropped passes, a knock-on and some missed tackles. But there was also genius. There was something special about Campese. His trademark 'goosestep' thrilled the Christchurch crowd. In fact, the whole country had been introduced to the brash young Australian and, quite unbelievably, they liked what they saw.

"When New Zealand rugby people accept you, you know you are doing all right," says Campese. "To be able to go to New Zealand and feel respected is something very special to me. I think I am respected in New Zealand because I would do things that their players wouldn't. If I had to go one-on-one with Stu Wilson they'd want to see Stu win every time but nevertheless the respect has always been there.

"Even in 1982, I could sense that the people liked what they saw – although I couldn't understand all the attention the 'goosestep' would get. It had been a part of my game since I was eight! But after I'd done it in a test everyone went overboard about it. It's not like I was the only guy doing it. I learned it by watching a league player do it... but in New Zealand it was the talk of the town."

When the Wallabies assembled in Wellington for the second test it was largely agreed that the All Blacks would secure the series win against the young Australian side. In fact, before leaving Australia for New Zealand, Dwyer and his management team had been quick to remind everyone that the tour was very much a rebuilding one. Winning was not necessarily a key... reshaping the Wallabies was the goal.

And who could blame him? This All Black side were arguably better than the New Zealand side that would win the inaugural World Cup five years later. The front row were one of the best to don the All Black jersey with Andy Dalton flanked by Gary Knight and John Ashworth. The loose forward trio of Graham Mourie, Murray Mexted and Mark Shaw was a combination of raw strength, speed and power and in Andy Haden the All Blacks had a lock who could all but guarantee lineout ball. Halfback Dave Loveridge's combination with first-five Wayne Smith was blossoming and the Wellington back three of Allan Hewson, Bernie Fraser and Stu Wilson was unquestionably the best back three combo in rugby.

"There was no way we were going to win that game," says Campese. "That All Black team was so strong that no one gave us a chance. Maybe the Australian team that had beaten Scotland earlier in the year may have had a chance at upsetting them, but not this Wallaby team. We were a team packed with a bunch of kids who should have been shaking in their boots."

Astonishingly, the Australians won. In time the 19-16 win would be seen as the day that Australian rugby was reborn. At the time it was declared as a miraculous win for the Wallabies and as one of the blackest days in New Zealand rugby.

Says Campese: "Talk about being in a state of shock. No one had tipped us to win. Nobody! We were playing a New Zealand side that was on a different level to us. We were playing a New Zealand side that had years of proud history to call on. We had none. Yet we'd beaten them by playing running rugby. We'd taken on their forward dominating style, and beaten them. Remarkable."

Campese had delivered the final pass for Gary Ella to score before he touched down himself to help the Australians to a 19-3 halftime lead. The All Blacks fought back valiantly in the second half but Dwyer's men weren't about to let this rare opportunity slip away. It was Australia's first win on New Zealand soil since 1978, when in the "dead" test at Eden Park Wallaby No 8 Greg Cornelsen scored four tries in a 30-16 win.

"I don't know if I appreciated the win as much as I should have," says Campese. "Of course, I was thrilled that we'd beaten the All Blacks but if I'd known that I was going to be on the end of a few beatings in the next few years I'd probably have kept celebrating for a few more weeks. That All Black side was a very good one... unfortunately, they'd remind us of that a couple of weeks later."

The All Blacks clinched the series with a 33-18 victory at Eden Park. Roger Gould's opening-minute try had served as a wake-up call for Mourie's men who went on to score two tries as they dominated the young Wallabies. The New Zealanders' dominance was pressed home by Hewson, who scored a world record 26 points with a try, two conversions, five penalty goals and a dropped goal.

"The thing that makes the All Blacks great is their ability to react under pressure," says Campese. "It doesn't matter how much pressure they are under, there always seems to be someone on the track that can get them out of trouble. Obviously, they don't win every game all of the time, but more often than not they manage to get themselves out of the fire.

"The pressure on that All Black team was huge. After they'd lost the second test I was amazed how the feeling of the country changed. They were calling for the players' blood. The fans demanded success in Auckland and the All Blacks delivered it. A lot of sides would have crumbled under that sort of pressure. But not those guys. Australian rugby may have come of age in Wellington, but we'd been put in our place in Auckland."

&

WHEN a player is as skilful as David Campese, there is a tendency to believe that all the player has is skill. Things come easier to him... coaches treat him more leniently... he doesn't have to work as hard as the others ...

Campese had the skill. His ability to make something out of nothing remains unmatched. His speed and his ability to elude defenders sent editors reaching for a thesaurus – unique, unequalled, alone, incomparable, matchless, peerless, unrivalled. But Campese had something greater than skill; something that he would need to prove in 1986.

By the time he arrived in New Zealand for the three-test tour, the world was acquainted with him. Everyone knew that Campese could turn a match in an instant. They knew of his frailties as well. Campese played his rugby the way he lived his life. It was all about taking risks.

"Sometimes you have got to try the unexpected simply because it is the unexpected," he says. "If I am being marked by a player who thinks he knows what I am going to do, and I do it, what chance have I got? I think I would have been a pretty boring player if I didn't take the odd risk. I would have been a good player, but not a great player. Okay, so sometimes I've tried to pick the ball up with one hand instead of two and knocked on. Sometimes I've thought about what I want to do before I get the ball and then when the ball is passed to me I drop the ball. So what? I didn't score 64 test tries by being your average run-of-the-mill winger."

Campese's selection at fullback for the first test was in many ways a risk by Wallaby coach Alan Jones. While he had been successful there during Argentina's tour to Australia weeks earlier, many thought Campese's limitations in defence could be found out against the All Blacks. But Jones was undeterred. His air of confidence in Campese at the beginning of the series was akin to the confidence that ran right through the Wallaby camp.

Things had changed since 1982. The Wallabies were no longer the poor cousins of the Tasman Sea. In 1984 Jones had led them on a tour of the United Kingdom where wins were secured against England, Wales, Ireland and Scotland – the Grand Slam. There had been victories against the All Blacks as well. In 1984 Australia had beaten New Zealand 16-9 in Sydney before going on to lose the series. And in 1985 there was further evidence the gap between the two countries had closed when the All Blacks needed a sensational try from winger Craig Green to escape with a 10-9 win at Eden Park in a one-off test.

The All Blacks were forced to go into the first test of the 1986 series without nine first-choice players. Cavaliers returning from the tour to South Africa were banned by the New Zealand Rugby Union for two tests. The first of those tests was won by the Baby Blacks 18-9 against France. But there were strong doubts that David Kirk could rally his troops against the hardened Wallabies.

Campese blew the game open midway through the first half when he collected a pass from halfback Nick Farr-Jones before kicking ahead and touching down for the try. He also played a part in the second Australian try, making the decisive pass to Matt Burke to help secure a 13-12 Wallaby win.

"People still like to question the value of that win," says Campese. "They talk about the Baby Blacks and how we would have struggled if the old guard had been allowed to play in the test. As far as I am concerned that's bullshit. No one can tell me that was a weak All Black side. They proved they were a good side when they beat the French.

"I don't care how many of the senior guys were missing because I know that at no time in the history of the All Blacks has there been a dud. Any player who pulls on that black jersey can play rugby. The depth of strength in New Zealand rugby is phenomenal. It's not as though they had to search high and low for 15 guys. Just look at some of the names that played that day: John Kirwan, Joe Stanley, David Kirk, Mike Brewer, Sean Fitzpatrick... not exactly duds are they?"

Following the loss, the New Zealand selectors wasted no time in reintroducing nine of the Cavaliers to the test side for the game in Dunedin. Mike Brewer was the only forward to retain his place and that was only because Wayne Shelford, who had been selected to play, broke a bone in his hand in a club game. The only other Baby Blacks to survive the axe were first-five Frano Botica, centre Joe Stanley and fullback Greg Cooper. David Kirk and John Kirwan – long-standing All Blacks who didn't tour with the Cavaliers – were joined by a star-studded cast that included Steve McDowell, Hika Reid, Gary Knight, Gary Whetton, Murray Pierce, Jock Hobbs, Alan Whetton, Warwick Taylor and Craig Green.

The gamble by the All Black selectors paid off... just. David Kirk scored the game's solitary try in helping to secure a 13-12 win, although the Wallabies felt they had been robbed when a Steve Tuynman try was disallowed by Welsh referee Derek Bevan. Indeed, the Wallabies could have won the game in the final minute but Michael Lynagh's dropped goal attempt sailed wide. But the drama on the field was nothing like the scene that was played out under Carisbrook's main stand in the Australian shed.

Tension between Alan Jones and David Campese had been growing throughout the tour. Campese disliked Jones' dictatorial manner. The coach, while a good motivator, would often talk down to his players. After the 10-9 loss to New Zealand a year earlier at Eden Park he had called his players *my stupid little dimwits* because they'd allowed the break that led to the game-winning try by Craig Green. And on this occasion it was Campese who would be singled out for special attention from Jones.

Campese hadn't had a good game. He had dropped a few up-and-unders and his mistakes led to long periods of All Black pressure. While Campese was showering after the game, Jones was heard to say to some of the Wallabies still in the changing area, "Don't worry fellows, you played without a fullback today." Campese heard about the comment from a teammate two days later.

This was Campese's challenge. The winger, arguably the best in the world at the time, was at his lowest point. Neither the goosestep nor the lethal pace could save him now. The time was right for Campese to prove his mental toughness. The time was right for him to prove that he could overcome the self-doubt. The time was right for him to prove that he could overcome Alan Jones' doubt.

"No one goes out there to play badly," he says. "Every time I pull on the Wallaby jersey I want to play the best game I've ever played. That's how important it is to me. I'd let myself down in Dunedin and I wanted to put things right in Auckland. I didn't feel like I had the support of my coach so I had to look within myself."

Campese didn't need to look too far for motivation. He had become a great admirer of the All Black ethos, the tradition imprinted in every New Zealander who plays rugby.

"People have often asked me what it is that makes the All Blacks so special. We've all heard of the intrigue and mysticism that goes with the black jersey. But the greatest thing is the All Black attitude. It's a refuse-to-lose mentality. I hate losing as much as anyone but once a game is over I can usually dissociate myself from it and get on with life.

"The All Blacks seem to feel the losses more. The country is so proud of anyone who becomes an All Black it is as though the players feel that they are letting down every player who has ever worn the black jersey when they lose. An All Black is never just playing for himself or the team. They are playing for New Zealand. In many ways that is a phenomenal pressure. But it must be a real motivation as well. Imagine having all of Australia behind you... knowing that everyone in the country is watching. That has got to be hugely inspiring."

To help motivate himself for the third test Campese needed only to think about what he was on the verge of. Australia had not won a series in New Zealand since 1949, when Johnny Smith captained an All Black side without the country's top 30 players who were on tour in South Africa... in many ways it was the impossible dream.

"Going to New Zealand and beating the All Blacks was not the sort of thing that was supposed to happen. To beat them in a one-off test takes the kind of discipline that is not required when you play any other country. To beat them in a series... well, that was going to take a monumental effort. But there was a belief among the team that we could do it.

"We certainly didn't have an inferiority complex about them. In the past I think a few teams have gone into a test match against the All Blacks convinced that they shouldn't even be on the same field. But an inferiority complex against the All Blacks is completely useless. You might as well not even bother turning up for the game. We felt like we belonged. We'd proven in the first test that the All Blacks were beatable and the referee cheated us out of the win in Dunedin. So we were ready for the battle. But we knew the All Blacks would be ready as well."

Campese was dropped from the fullback's role and moved to the right wing where he replaced Peter Grigg. Andrew Leeds, who replaced Campese at fullback, helped the Australians to a 12-6 halftime lead when he scored a try after some good build-up work from second-five Brett Papworth. The All Blacks, perhaps inspired by the open-running style of rugby preached by Alan Jones, ran the ball at the Australians at every opportunity as they tried to fight their way back into the series decider. But try as they might the New Zealanders couldn't breach the Wallaby line.

When the Australians regained the momentum late in the second half Nick Farr-Jones took control. His darting runs from the base of the scrum had the All Blacks' loose forwards Jock Hobbs, Mike Brewer and Mark Shaw scrambling right to the end of the test when, with two minutes remaining, he broke from a maul before passing to Campese who scored the series-clinching try. The Wallabies had won the Bledisloe Cup for the first time since 1980, and for the first time on New Zealand soil for 37 years.

"The Grand Slam in 1984 was something very special but in many ways, this topped that," says Campese. "Beating the All Blacks at any time is a career highlight. Beating them in a series in New Zealand is just awesome.

"Not many New Zealanders had too much time for us on that tour. Even before the third test you could sense that the public and the press hated Alan Jones. Obviously, I had a few run-ins with him but Jonesy knew what he wanted and how he wanted to achieve it. There was a certain arrogance about the Australian sides that he coached.

"In many ways it was similar to what we'd been used to seeing from the All Blacks. At times the All Blacks get a bit carried away with the arrogant side of things but generally it is acceptable. You have to be a bit arrogant to play at the highest level of any sport. You have to believe that you are better than the other guy. It's the only way you can be successful. That doesn't mean you have to be a prick. You can still be a nice guy... it's just that, when it comes to rugby, you're the man. We had that aura about us. We'd only just found it as a team. The All Blacks had had it for years."

&

THIS was a strange occurrence. After everything that had gone before – the enormous highs of victory and the tragedy of the lows – David Campese should have known better. He reminded himself that you should never write off an All Black team. After all, it was only a year after the home-series loss to Australia that the All Blacks lifted the World Cup. And things hadn't exactly gone according to the Wallaby plan since. There was the 3-0 whitewash in 1988, the one-off test loss in 1989 and the 2-1 series defeat in 1990.

But Campese refused to budge. As he sat in the changing rooms at Eden Park after a dour 6-3 New Zealand win in 1991, he was convinced Australia would win the World Cup later that year.

Everything he'd learned about the All Blacks since making his debut against them in 1982 suddenly stood for nothing. The All Black aura... gone. The respect for the All Blacks... wavering.

"It was the first and last time that I knew we could beat the All Blacks," says Campese. "It was obvious to me that that All Black side was at the end of the road. Some of the more experienced guys had hung on one or two seasons too long and it was beginning to show. You could sense that they had very little left in the tank. They relied on the goalkicking of Grant Fox. If Foxy had a good day they would be competitive. If the chances didn't come his way they were like a lame duck. Time had caught up with them."

The warning signs for the All Blacks had first surfaced during the Wallaby tour in 1990. Bob Dwyer – back in charge of the Australian side – had guided his team to the third test win in Wellington. That was followed up with a 21-12 win against the All Blacks in Sydney before the kicking duel in Auckland between Michael Lynagh and Grant Fox.

"We'd thumped them in Sydney and the All Blacks offered nothing new at Eden Park," says Campese. "We still respected them but any fear that some of the guys may have had of them in the past was long gone. They'd lost the plot a bit off the field as well. They were still acting like they were unbeatable when they weren't. I know you need a little bit of arrogance to be successful in sport but they took it too far.

"They made some very silly decisions off the field once they got to the World Cup. They charged people £1 to watch them train. It was ridiculous. They were a team on the slide but instead of trying to figure out what to do to stop the slide they were trying to figure out ways to make money. The fans remember things like that. They didn't do anything to endear themselves to the local fans."

The Australians targeted the semifinal as their World Cup final right from the outset of the 1991 tournament. They cruised through their pool games against Argentina, Western Samoa and Wales before a scare against Ireland in the quarter-finals when they needed a late try from Michael Lynagh to escape with a 19-18 victory.

"Once we knew we were in the semis we knew we were only a game away from being the world champions," says Campese. "It didn't matter that a final still had to be played... we were convinced that whoever beat New Zealand would win the tournament. We were confident we could do it, too. As far as I could tell the All Blacks hadn't progressed since the Eden Park test. We knew they'd do the basic things well but I couldn't see how they were going to beat us. We'd saved ourselves during the tournament for that game. We were as ready as we were ever going to be."

Campese was the unequivocal star of the semifinal. In the 12th minute of the game he drifted in off the blindside wing to receive a pass and headed towards the opposite corner, turning John Kirwan inside-out in the process.

"As soon as I got the ball in my hands I knew what I wanted to do. I did everything that the coaches tell you not to do. I headed crossfield and just went for the corner. At one stage I saw Phil Kearns outside me and thought, *Oh shit, I'm not going pass him the bloody ball*. I was quick enough to get to the line. It was a magic moment."

Six minutes before halftime Campese was at it again. Chasing a kick from Michael Lynagh, he gathered the ball, evaded All Black fullback Kieran Crowley and threw a blind pass over his shoulder which Tim Horan took before crashing over the line. The semifinal was effectively over before halftime. Australia would eventually win 16-6 and a week later defeated England 12-6 in the final at Twickenham.

While Campese would play another seven tests against the All Blacks, no moment was to match the highs from the semifinal at Dublin's Lansdowne Road. Former Irish first-five Tony Ward was so moved by Campese's performance that day that he said, "He is the Maradona, the Pele, of international rugby all rolled into one. You can't put a value on his importance to our game. He is a breath of fresh air and I think perhaps the greatest player of all time."

Indeed, Campese's try that day is the most replayed Campo Moment on highlight reels across the world. The fact that it was his good friend and rival John Kirwan who was on the receiving end made it all the more special.

"When you are playing at the highest level of any sport you want to test yourself against the best," he says. "If you score a try against the United States team it's a nice feeling but if you score against a guy like John Kirwan then it's a great feeling. I have a tremendous amount of respect for JK. There is no question that he was a great winger but he could have been so much better if the All Blacks got the ball to him more. A lot of times he was starved of possession. When you have an asset like that on your wing you should make it a priority to get him the ball. I don't care how good your forwards are, it's a waste of talent not putting the ball in his hands."

During his 29 tests against the All Blacks Campese played against some of the great All Black wingers. But Kirwan stands out as the best ahead of the likes of Stu Wilson, Craig Green, Terry Wright, Inga Tuigamala, Jonah Lomu and Jeff Wilson.

"JK was so strong. He would have been absolutely lethal if you'd put him in a Wallaby jersey. We had a great forward pack in those days but the backline was unmatched. JK would have loved playing outside guys like Tim Horan and Jason Little."

The two wingers would renew their rivalry the year after the World Cup when the All Blacks toured Australia. And again it would be Campese who would come out smiling. In the first test at Sydney, Kirwan had an opportunity to win the game for the All Blacks but he knocked on when all he had to do was pick up a loose ball and fall over the line. As the teams left the field after the Wallabies had held on to win 16-15 Campo sought Kirwan out. *Bad luck mate, but thank God you dropped it.*

The Australians would go on to win the series with a 19-17 win at Ballymore in Brisbane before the All Blacks claimed the third test with a 26-23 win. It had been one of the most entertaining series of the modern era. The two first five eighths – Grant Fox and Michael Lynagh – provided the difference between the two teams, with each scoring two tries in each outing. But unlike the Eden

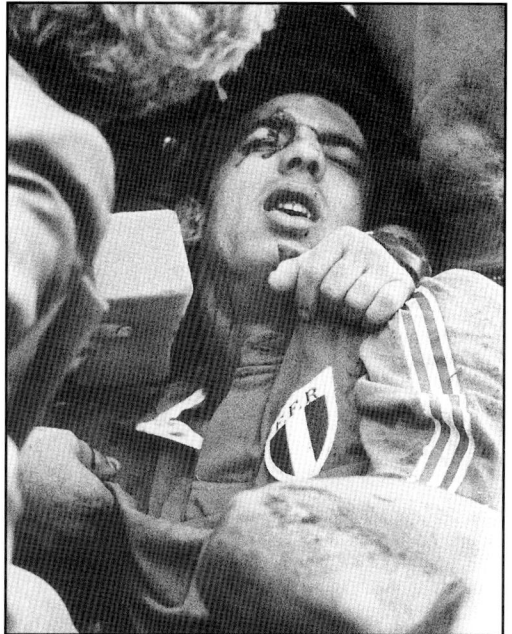

Welcome to New Zealand...
Serge Blanco was knocked
unconscious against Counties in
the last match of France's short
tour in 1984.

French skipper Pierre Berbizier screams up in support as Serge Blanco
attacks against the All Blacks during the Tricolores' two-test tour of New
Zealand in 1989.

A youthful David Campese leaves All Black flanker Jock Hobbs (on ground) and first-five Ian Dunn in his wake during the 1983 one-off Bledisloe Cup test in Sydney. Despite the Campese capers, New Zealand won this match 18-8.

Dawie de Villiers heads for the goalline and a try against NZ Maori at Athletic Park during the Springboks' tour of New Zealand in 1965. The hapless New Zealand Maori defender is Sid Going. De Villiers' men won this match 9-3.

Happiness is... Dawie de Villiers (left) and team-mates Jannie Engelbrecht, Sakkie van Zyl and Don Walton celebrate the Springboks' third test win over New Zealand at Lancaster Park. After being down 5-16 at halftime South Africa came back to win this match 19-16.

Dawie de Villiers is lifted high on the shoulders of rapturous South African supporters after the Boks' first test win over the All Blacks at Pretoria in 1970. De Villiers led South Africa to a 3-1 series victory.

Gareth Edwards gets his pass away in front of arch rival Sid Going during the second test of the 1971 series between the British Isles and New Zealand at Christchurch. The All Blacks' 22-12 victory was their sole win in the series.

Disconsolate captain Gavin Hastings walks off Eden Park with New Zealand skipper Sean Fitzpatrick after the Lions' third test – and series-deciding – loss to the All Blacks in 1993.

Baptism of Black fire... Phil Kearns shows off the "full teapot" during his test debut against the All Blacks at Eden Park in 1989. The Wallabies lost this match 12-24, but Kearns would exact sweet revenge many times over in the 1990s.

There have been few greater rivalries in world rugby than the titanic duels fought between Willie John McBride and Colin Meads. Here McBride appears to have the edge over the great "Pinetree" during the 1971 All Blacks-Lions series.

Park test of 1991, both teams wanted to play an open style of rugby. It was something the Wallabies had been doing since Bob Dwyer had taken charge of the team in 1982. New Zealand had to wait for the introduction of Laurie Mains, who emerged as the All Black coach out of the ashes of Dublin, before a commitment to open rugby came.

"It was the best series I've been involved in against the All Blacks," says Campese. "Obviously winning in New Zealand in 1986 was a bigger deal in terms of the achievement, but the style of rugby that both teams played in 1992 made it memorable.

"It's the sort of series that we aren't likely to see again either. In those days, when you showed up at the ground you could be sure that you were going to see the ball moved through the backline. The Australian fans could be sure that Nick Farr-Jones would supply quick ball to Michael Lynagh who would get it out to Tim Horan and Jason Little who would feed the wingers and the fullback.

"The All Blacks got into the spirit as well with guys like Grant Fox, Walter Little and Frank Bunce intent on getting the ball to players like John Kirwan, John Timu and Inga Tuigamala. Both teams wanted to run the ball. If you watch a tape of those tests it's obvious that everyone was enjoying their football. It was tough rugby, bloody tough, but both teams were prepared to take a few risks. It was attacking rugby... the exact opposite of what we're served up these days.

"The game has become too negative. Players are playing shit rugby because coaches are too scared to run the ball. Look at current Australian coach Rod Macqueen. He is paranoid about losing. He has taken the flair and skill out of the Australian backline and replaced it with crashers. Training sessions are dominated by defensive drills. What about attack? What about playing with a bit of flair?

"There's no doubt that the skill levels of the players playing these days aren't up to the skill levels of the guys that I used to play with and against. It's happening all over the world. Today's players are better athletes. And so they should be with all the time they spend in the gymnasium but skill-wise, I'm afraid, they don't hold a candle to many of the guys who have gone before them.

"Joe Roff is incredible! How many times have we seen the guy drop the ball? When I was playing you were terrified of dropping the ball because if you did you were dropped. Now it's just an accepted part of the game.

"It's a shame because when rugby is played the way it was in 1992 there is nothing that comes close to competing with it. When it's played right it's the greatest game in the world. When it's played the way it was played during the Bledisloe Cup test in Sydney in 1999, it's a bore. Who wants to watch Matthew Burke kick penalty after penalty? Where's the enjoyment in that? Australia won the game but how many of the 107,000 people who watched the game walked out of the stadium excited about what they saw?"

ða

HE is no longer the centre of attention. He has played his last test, scored his last try. But the battle to help Australian rugby reach the level of the All Blacks goes on.

"My interest now lies in trying to convince people that the traditions of the Wallabies are worth celebrating," he says. "If Australian rugby is going to go from strength to strength we have to take a look at what makes All Black rugby so great. I'm not just talking about what happens on the field. The All Blacks dominated the Bledisloe Cup between 1988 and 1990. It was Australia's turn between 1991 and 1995. Then the All Blacks dominated again until 1998 when the Australians cleaned them out 3-0. Eras will come and go. There are a lot of things that have to happen off the field. New Zealand is still miles ahead of us there."

Ever since Otago halfback James Duncan captained New Zealand against Australia in 1903 New Zealanders have put the All Blacks on a pedestal. All Blacks of a bygone era continue to hold a fascination with the New Zealand public even though many of the worshippers never saw the likes of Dave Gallaher, George Nepia, Fred Allen, Colin Meads, Wilson Whineray or Brian Lochore take the world's rugby fields.

"It was those sorts of blokes who built up the great All Black myth," says Campese. "They are the ones responsible for the fear that the current All Blacks put into some of their opponents. You hear stories about the All Blacks being bigger and stronger than anyone else. It's rubbish, of course, but the myth survives. They have a rich tradition which is passed on from father to son. Generation after generation of New Zealanders never lose sight of the importance of the past.

"Australia has a proud past as well. We've had our great players through the years. But what chance have we got in building that sort of tradition when guys like Mark Ella and myself are already being cast to join the forgotten ones."

Campese, who played the last of his 101 tests against Wales in 1996, was made an official ambassador for Wallaby rugby in 1998 but the role was extinguished by the time the 1999 season began. After captaining the Australian Sevens team to a bronze medal at the 1998 Commonwealth Games, Campese applied for the sevens' coaching job which had been vacated by Mark Ella.

"The first thing they asked me when I went for the interview was *How do you get along with Rod Macqueen?* What has that got to do with coaching sevens? I knew straight away that I wasn't going to get the job. There are so many paranoid people in Australian rugby. Macqueen didn't let Mark have access to the top Wallaby players for the Commonwealth Games because he knew if Mark had been successful the pressure would have come on to him to match that success in fifteens. I'm sure paranoia had something to do with me missing out on the sevens job as well. The Australian Rugby Union don't like me because I'm outspoken. They don't like the fact that I express my opinions and ideas.

"The administrators have got to catch up with New Zealand and realise that now that the game has gone professional they have to take a step backwards. There are very few administrators doing things for the good of the game at the moment. Most of them are still in it for themselves."

Campese cites the ARU's decision to allow changes to the Wallaby jersey as a sign of how out-of-touch Australia's administrators are.

During the battle for control of the future of the game between the Kerry Packer-backed World Rugby Corporation and Rupert Murdoch-backed SANZAR, the ARU pleaded with its players to stay true to the traditions of Wallaby rugby. "They told us not to sell out the past," says Campese, "and the next thing they do is change the jersey. We had players making their debut for Australia saying that the new jersey was shit. Can you imagine the All Blacks changing the design of their jersey that drastically? It would never happen. It was just another sign of how far we have to go before we catch up."

There's no doubt Campese is envious when he looks to former opponents like Andy Dalton, Wayne Smith, Graham Mourie, Wayne Shelford and Grant Fox – players who have all graduated to high-profile coaching or administrative positions.

"I want to help Australian rugby," he says. "I would do anything I could to help the development of the game. It would be much easier to play a part in the future of rugby if I had been an All Black. If I'd worn that black jersey I know that someone in New Zealand would be giving me an outlet to express myself. The ridiculous fact is that I can go to Singapore, Japan, Europe or America and coach but I can't get a job in Australia. How are we ever going to progress if we can't accommodate the players who have built up Australian rugby since 1982, let alone the guys who preceded us? The Kiwis must be having a good old laugh."

DAVID CAMPESE AGAINST THE ALL BLACKS

Date	For	Venue	Result	Score	Points
14-8-82	Australia	Christchurch	lost	16-23	try
28-8-82	Australia	Wellington	won	19-16	try
11-9-82	Australia	Auckland	lost	18-33	
20-8-83	Australia	Sydney	lost	8-18	
21-7-84	Australia	Sydney	won	16-9	
25-7-84	ACT	Canberra	lost	16-40	dg
4-8-84	Australia	Brisbane	lost	15-19	pen
18-8-84	Australia	Sydney	lost	24-25	try, pen
9-8-86	Australia	Wellington	won	13-12	try
23-8-86	Australia	Dunedin	lost	12-13	
6-9-86	Australia	Auckland	won	22-9	try
25-7-87	Australia	Sydney	lost	16-30	
22-6-88	Randwick	Sydney	lost	9-25	
3-7-88	Australia	Sydney	lost	7-32	
16-7-88	Australia	Brisbane	drew	19-19	
23-7-88	NSW	Sydney	lost	6-42	
30-7-88	Australia	Sydney	lost	9-30	
5-8-89	Australia	Auckland	lost	12-24	try
21-7-90	Australia	Christchurch	lost	6-21	
4-8-90	Australia	Auckland	lost	17-27	
18-8-90	Australia	Wellington	won	21-9	
10-8-91	Australia	Sydney	won	21-12	
24-8-91	Australia	Auckland	lost	3-6	
27-10-91	Australia	Dublin	won	16-6	try
4-7-92	Australia	Sydney	won	16-15	try
19-7-92	Australia	Brisbane	won	19-17	
25-7-92	Australia	Sydney	lost	23-26	
17-7-93	Australia	Dunedin	lost	10-25	
17-8-94	Australia	Sydney	won	20-16	
29-7-95	Australia	Sydney	lost	23-34	
6-7-96	Australia	Wellington	lost	6-43	
27-7-96	Australia	Brisbane	lost	25-32	

TEST MATCH CAREER

	P	W	L	D	T	C	P	Dg	Pts
vs All Blacks	29	10	18	1	8	-	3	-	42
All Tests	101	67	32	2	64	8	7	2	315

Dawie de Villiers

Date of birth: 10-7-1940
Born at: Burgersdorp,
 South Africa
Position: Halfback
Test matches: 25

"Dawie de Villiers was an outstanding scrumhalf whose speed and incisiveness compensated for the occasional lapses in his service... courage, both physical and moral, was always to be his strongest attribute on and off the field"

Chris Greyvenstein
(Springbok Saga, 1981)

Charles Dickens' classic opening line from A Tale of Two Cities, "It was the best of times, it was the worst of times..." could have been penned with the 1965 Springboks in mind.

Dawie de Villiers' South African side had defeated the All Blacks hours earlier at Christchurch's Lancaster Park. It should have been one of those magic moments in a Springbok career that a player looks back on and cherishes. The enemy had been defeated. It was what he'd dreamt about achieving and, for a while at least, he revelled in the glory.

But it wasn't long before a shadow was cast over the South Africans in an incident which would set the tone for bitter debates between the two countries for years to come, culminating in the violent and ill-conceived 1981 Springbok tour.

"We were ready to celebrate a fantastic achievement," says de Villiers. "We had beaten the All Blacks. It had been the culmination of a lot of hard work and a lot of soul-searching. It had promised to be a night of great celebration."

While the South Africans were still recounting the stories from the thrilling 19-16 win, news of a statement from their Prime Minister, Hendrik Verwoerd, broke from the republic which effectively said that there would be no Maori allowed in the All Black team that were due to tour South Africa two years later.

"It turned into a very dark day for us," says de Villiers. "We gathered that evening and we felt embarrassed. There we were, playing in this country – playing against Maori and getting along with them very well – and there was the Prime Minister telling New Zealanders that some of you are welcome in 1967 and some of you are not. It was a very unpleasant day for us. It certainly had an effect on the tour.

"I got together with manager Kobus Louw and we talked to the players. It was very clear that regardless of whether they were supporters of the government or people who did not support them, there was absolute unanimity among all the players that this was a very unfortunate development.

"I was very frustrated at the statements coming from South Africa. As players we wanted to be tested against the best All Black side possible. There would be no joy in defeating an All Black side that did not include men like Waka Nathan or Bryan Williams. But regardless of what would or wouldn't happen on the field, I was left with a feeling of embarrassment. I didn't have a problem looking someone like Waka in the eye after that night because he knew my feelings about Hendrik Verwoerd. But you could sense some bitterness towards the team from some sections of the New Zealand public. To this day I don't blame them. It was an unfortunate incident that determined politics and rugby would become intertwined in the years ahead."

&.

THERE was no hiding place. It was the first tour to New Zealand since the brutal series in 1956 when New Zealand beat South Africa in a series for the first time. That South African team had returned home in disgrace and as Dawie de Villiers' side prepared for the tour they were left in no doubt they were carrying the hopes of a nation as they ventured to New Zealand.

Before the team left for the four-test tour de Villiers and his charges were inundated with advice from members of the 1956 side – men like Jan Pickard and Jan du Preez.

"Before we even got to New Zealand, every player was aware that there was a tremendous rivalry between South Africa and New Zealand on the rugby fields," says de Villiers. "Both countries had a great rugby tradition, they were proud of their teams. It was one way in which they could stand up in the world and really show themselves.

"Behind the scenes there was a tremendous build-up to the tour. The experience of one tour was passed on to the next. When the players from the 1956 tour visited us you could sense that, for them, our tour was a continuation of their visit to New Zealand. There was still a lot of bitterness among some of the players that they lost that series. They had put the record straight when they had beaten the All Blacks in South Africa in 1960 but the unfinished business on New Zealand soil remained.

"The motivation within the team by the time we left for New Zealand couldn't have been stronger... the past Springboks wouldn't have had it any other way! They told us to prepare for war. They'd say, 'New Zealand is a wonderful place to tour and the people are very friendly... but the friendship ends on the rugby field. The All Blacks will do anything to win. They will be nasty. They will be shrewd. They will stop at nothing to beat us.'

"It was marvellous to have their support. Today, with tours leaving every other month, there is not the same camaraderie between the old players and the new. But in 1965 a tour to New Zealand was one of the events of your life.

"To be selected to go on a Springbok tour to New Zealand was the greatest thrill. Playing against the All Blacks – even in South Africa – would have seemed like the highest possible achievement. But going to New Zealand... this was the ultimate."

To understand the weight of expectations on the 26-year-old

captain's shoulders you must first acknowledge de Villiers' passion for the long-standing relationship between New Zealand and South Africa.

This was a man who was brought up on stories about the great rivalry. During the 1956 tour de Villiers would scan newspapers, hungry for every column inch of news from New Zealand. He would read about men like Kevin Skinner, Don Clarke and Peter Jones. He would be disturbed to read that his heroes had no answer to the All Black juggernaut that would claim the series 3-1. A Springbok side had never lost to the All Blacks before that. In 1921 – with South African legends like Boy Morkel and Phil Mostert starring – the Boks had drawn a three-test series in New Zealand 1-1, with one match drawn, before the return series seven years later was tied at 2-2. When the sides met in New Zealand again in 1937 the Springboks triumphed 2-1 before sweeping Fred Allen's All Blacks 4-0 in 1949.

While many of the All Blacks' challengers of this era would talk about being in awe of the New Zealanders, this certainly wasn't the case when it came to this rivalry. The All Blacks may have had men like George Nepia, Kevin Skinner, Wilson Whineray and Colin Meads striking fear into their opponents but the Springboks had a long line of legends who had not only fronted up to the All Blacks, they had defeated them regularly.

"I hear of players from other countries talking about the All Blacks as though they were gods," says de Villiers. "That is something I can't understand. Of course, the All Blacks are to be respected. But for every great All Black there has been a great Springbok. We knew that touring New Zealand was going to be the toughest assignment of our careers but we were looking forward to it. Was it daunting? Absolutely. Was there fear? Absolutely not.

"The tradition between the two countries ensured that there was a tremendous respect between the two teams. It was an honour for every young boy in New Zealand or South Africa to think of himself as an All Black or a Springbok. It was a duty to play the game, and if you got the honour to play for your country it was so much more important.

"Regardless of the rivalry – and at times it was like a bloody war – there was always great respect between the countries for one another. We admired the great All Blacks and I am sure they looked with admiration to many of the great Springboks that we have produced and that is an important perspective because although we had fierce battles on the field, we could go off and retain respect for each other.

"There were incidents, that's true. It was a very physical game, it was a hard game. There was no room for moaners and groaners. You had to take it or leave it and both teams could give it and take it. It was the way rugby should be played.

"I hear players talking today about how they had fun out there on the field. Let me tell you something, when I played rugby against New Zealand it was never fun. The fun came after the game. When you were playing a test you had to play it as though your life depended on it. You owed that to every Springbok and every All Black who had played before you because there had been bitterness and some animosity in the past. There were elements of love – respect and admiration – and elements of hate. The All Blacks were our enemy. They were the men we needed to overcome, the men we needed to slaughter. It was *never* fun."

By the time of the first test at Wellington's Athletic Park, de Villiers' Boks were feeling the pressure a New Zealand tour provides. In the second match of the tour they had been beaten by Wellington 23-6.

"There is no doubt we felt the weight of the past resting on our shoulders," says de Villiers. "The loss to Wellington didn't affect us greatly but there were certainly no positives to come out of it. If anything, it intensified the great expectation of our country and our supporters. We knew everyone was demanding us to win but at the same time we knew we were facing an almost impossible task. But, beating New Zealand in New Zealand... this was our mission. It was a challenge – whether we failed or succeeded – that we would be judged on for the rest of our lives."

The All Blacks went into the test without the retired Don Clarke and DJ Graham and the injured Waka Nathan and Malcolm Dick. With the Boks boasting five players who had played in the 1960 series in South Africa (won by South Africa 2-1) – Lofty Nel, Abe Malan, Lionel Wilson, Keith Oxlee and the brilliant centre John Gainsford – there was no over-confidence among the New Zealanders.

Despite impressive defence from the tourists, two first-half tries, to winger Bill Birtwistle and flanker Kel Tremain, gave the All Blacks a 6-0 lead. Seven minutes into the second half a penalty by Oxlee cut the lead to three points. The Boks looked capable of scoring again when Gainsford broke free but All Black flanker Dick Conway saved the day with a desperation tackle and the test ended in a 6-3 win to New Zealand.

The match was marred by a controversial decision by North Auckland referee Pat Murphy who, in allowing Tremain's try, seemed to ignore a knock-on by Mick Williment, who delivered the final pass.

"New Zealanders love to blame their series losses in South Africa on South African referees," says de Villiers. "Well, I was the one who tackled Mick Williment and I am convinced the ball was knocked-on, so I can say the feeling about 'home-town' referees is mutual!

"But, I wouldn't say either South African or New Zealand referees were intentionally poor. Different interpretations led to many misunderstandings and a feeling that you had not been fairly treated by a referee. Perhaps some of them, given the same pressures the players were under, felt they couldn't give a penalty against the All Blacks right in front of their posts in the last 10 minutes of a test. Perhaps subconsciously the referees had a fear of blowing the whistle if it was going to disadvantage the home side. Whatever the reasons for the alleged mistakes, make no mistake that both countries suffered from incompetence from referees at different times."

Regardless of Murphy's decision, the Springboks knew they hadn't deserved to win the test. The All Black pack – which included the Meads brothers Colin and Stan, Brian Lochore and Wilson Whineray – had been dominant. It was a worrying sign for the Boks – the same sign de Villiers had read about in 1956 when South Africa had been beaten in the first test on the way to a 1-3 series loss.

"They were a tremendous pack," he says. "It had been a very windy day but they played the conditions expertly. They kept the ball low and kept it within themselves. They had given us a rugby lesson but we'd kept the game close with some very good defence of our own.

"We certainly didn't feel after the game that we were thrashed or that it was a terrible defeat. Our confidence was dented, but we were not defeated before we played the second test. We were just more aware of the difficulties that we would have to face and the sacrifices we would have to make. To combat their pack, we would have to be much more confrontational."

The talk was spoken but the walk never eventuated in Dunedin where the Boks were handed a record 13-0 defeat. De Villiers had missed the test because of a cut eye picked up in the game against Auckland the previous weekend but he felt the pain of defeat as much as any of the Springbok XV. They had been outclassed. The heavy track at Carisbrook meant 10-man rugby was the order of the day and Whineray's men had carried on from Wellington and completely dominated the South Africans. With two tests to play, the best the Boks could hope for was a drawn series but, after this latest defeat, the biggest hurdle facing the South Africans was the prospect of a series whitewash.

As with any touring side, a losing team is usually a team with splinters running through it.

"It is always a problem on a tour when you have 30 players and some of them feel after a while they are only playing in the second-string side. And when the team is losing and they still aren't getting an opportunity to play, some players get disheartened. It was a difficult time... 0-2 down to the All Blacks with two tests to go isn't a place where any of us would like to go again.

"As the captain there was extra pressure on me but there's no point being dramatic... when you are in that situation you just have to deal with it. It's something the whole team had to face and I think I always tried to work on the team principle – a weight shared is a weight much lighter. So, sharing with my team the challenges, having a very open approach, allowing every player to contribute as to how he saw things and how we could deal with certain things helped us become a very close group of people on a mission.

"Of course there is tension, but once you have picked a team for a test like that and you start working on the preparation, then the basic instincts draw you together again.

"There was an urgency to win that third test. If nothing else we were driven by the knowledge that, if we didn't win, there was going to be tremendous disappointment among our own people. When you play for the Springboks, you play for your team, but you also play for your country. It was do or die for us. At the back of your mind was always the spectators, the crowds, the supporters in South Africa – you couldn't shake that off. The intensity for the game at home was an added pressure but it also provided encouragement because we knew the country was with us. The supporters in South Africa were standing at the crossroads with us."

With de Villiers restored to the test team, South Africa defeated the All Blacks 19-16 at Lancaster Park. They succeeded thanks largely to their ability to move the All Black pack around. Gainsford was at the top of his game as he scored two of the Springboks' four tries before Tiny Naude kicked a magnificent penalty out of the mud to secure the thrilling win.

"It was as though we'd had a gun to our heads," says de Villiers. "Rather than take the punishment we decided to fight back and the result was a famous victory. We answered the doubters. It was a victory that deserved a worthy celebration."

The celebration, cut short by Prime Minister Verwoerd's demands for the planned 1967 tour, was to be the last of the tour. Despite confidence being high going into the fourth test at Auckland's Eden Park, the Boks were handed their second record defeat of the tour as Whineray – who announced his retirement after the match – captained the New Zealanders to a 20-3 success.

"We'd gained a lot of confidence after the third test and we were rightly confident going into Auckland," says de Villiers. "We felt the team were right – we were fit, we believed we were focused... but we were not. Certainly, as the captain, it was not possible to get the same kind of focus and determination going as we had for the third test. As a result we contributed to our own defeat by making too many mistakes.

"We'd lost the series. We deserved to lose the series. We left New Zealand with sad hearts... but not because we were worried about the response we would get at home. The thing that worried us was that we'd set a target for ourselves. We had failed ourselves. That's the greatest failure. You can fail other people, but if you have failed yourself then you feel more disheartened.

"We had to go away and work on ourselves... you get beaten, you lie and bleed for a while, and then you gather yourself and you start the rebuilding process."

❧

SOMETIMES, when things go wrong, a sportsman begins to second-guess himself. Confidence is replaced by self-doubt and resolve gives way to a resignation that defeat is imminent.

In this case it wasn't a rugby player going through the crisis... it was a nation. For a country with as proud a record as South Africa has on the world's rugby fields, going into a series in the republic without the favourite's tag was unheard of. But that's the situation Dawie de Villiers faced when he prepared to lead his side against Brian Lochore's All Blacks in 1970.

Only six months earlier the Boks had returned from a demoralising northern hemisphere tour. Off the field, the South Africans for the first time came across massive demonstrations against their country's apartheid policies. With New Zealand cancelling the proposed 1967 tour because of the South African government's "No Maori" policy, people in Britain were incensed that the Springboks were being allowed to tour. The team were incarcerated in hotel rooms, unable to experience the pleasures that rugby tours normally would offer. On the field, the Boks failed to make their usual clean-sweep of Ireland, Scotland, England and Wales.

In contrast, the All Blacks had not been beaten in their last 17 tests – dating back to the third test loss to South Africa in 1965. A further endorsement of the All Blacks' might came when they won their first 10 tour games in South Africa.

"No one gave us a chance," says de Villiers. "And, to be honest, I don't really blame them. When you play against the All Blacks, you can never say with any great confidence that you will win. There is always an element of doubt. You can build your confidence, work on the ability of the team and improve your skills... but a win against the All Blacks is never guaranteed.

"With the disappointment of our northern hemisphere tour still fresh in our minds it was a difficult series to prepare for because leading up to the first test there was a definite feeling of self-doubt.

Some days when you play the All Blacks, you feel like you can compete but on other occasions you have to sit up straight and say *what are we going to do... we can't beat them.*"

The All Blacks, for the first time since 1964 – a run of 20 consecutive tests – were forced to go into an international without the services of Colin Meads, who had broken his forearm in the win against Eastern Transvaal. But despite Meads' absence there was still an experienced look to coach Ivan Vodanovich's side. Ian Kirkpatrick and Brian Lochore were as good as any loose forwards to have worn the black jersey, halfback Chris Laidlaw was third only to the Welsh No 9 Gareth Edwards and de Villiers in the battle for the world's best and the New Zealand backline boasted a hard-hitting midfield of Ian MacRae and Grahame Thorne and a debutant winger by the name of Bryan Williams. When the goalkicking expertise of Fergie McCormick is added, the task in front of the South Africans can be understood.

Once the Boks assembled and began their preparation for the opening test at Loftus Versfeld, de Villiers sensed a change in mood.

"Until we got together again there had been a strong negative feeling about playing the All Blacks. But once we came together there was a very strong resolve to win. Just as the 1956 Springboks had encouraged us before our departure for New Zealand in 1965, there was a feeling of unfinished business among this team carrying over from five years earlier. We had tasted defeat against the All Blacks and it wasn't pleasant. Come hell or high water, this time we would be the conquerors and the All Blacks would be the conquered.

"When we ran onto the field that day, we only had one thing on our minds. We were going to play our hearts out and if that was not good enough then nothing was good enough. The build-up was intense in the changing room. You work yourself to a point where you don't hear, you don't see, you don't speak. You just focus on this one thing that you want to do. It was probably the most focused team that that I have ever been a part of."

There have been many incidents throughout the history of tests between the Springboks and the All Blacks. *Brutal* is a word used to describe most of them, like the infamous incident at Eden Park in 1956 when Jaap Bekker kicked Tiny White in the spine, thinking the All Black lock was his propping rival Kevin Skinner. But on this day at Pretoria the Boks' brutality was all legal. Their tackling was brutal and their determination to attack the All Blacks disrupted the tourists' rhythm.

De Villiers and Sid Nomis scored tries as South Africa went one-up in the four-test series. Remarkably, the All Blacks were kept scoreless in the first half before a try from Williams and a penalty by McCormick offered some respectability to the final score of 17-6.

"The win was so special because it came against the backdrop of the disappointment of the lost series in 1965," says de Villiers. "It was also against the backdrop of the disaster of the northern hemisphere tour and the fact that very few commentators had given us even the slightest chance of winning the test. It really was a question of accomplishing the impossible."

De Villiers says his ability to unite a disillusioned Springbok squad before the test was in part down to the experience of 1965. "When you lose you must use that experience as a chance to learn. When I was in New Zealand it was like being at school. I wanted to learn as much as possible. I sought out as many former All Blacks as I could to talk to about the All Black ethos. I learned about the approach of the All Blacks. I learned about their training. And I had the chance to watch Wilson Whineray captain a side. I saw the way he led from the front. It was something I tried to adopt with my captaincy. I saw a lot in myself in the way Brian Lochore captained a team. He was a great tactician. He was always communicating with the forwards and the backs. He saw the game better than anyone I ever played against.

"Now to have beaten the All Blacks I had achieved a lifelong dream. I had led the Boks to a test win against New Zealand. As a youngster I'd studied the great All Black players. I'd read about their greatness and their skills. Some players I admired more than others. But on that day, I'd been a part of a South African side that had beaten a team that included great players like Lochore, Kirkpatrick and Laidlaw. It was a great thrill but the job wasn't done yet – 1970 was not just about getting a test win; it was all about striving for a series win."

The All Blacks found themselves in a similar situation as the Boks had been in five years earlier when they fronted up for the second test at Newlands. Desperate to avoid going 0-2 down, Vodanovich reintroduced Earle Kirton to the test line-up, replacing Wayne Cottrell in the No 10 jersey, while Alex Wyllie and Alan Sutherland were given their test debuts at the expense of Tom Lister and Alan Smith.

The changes worked as tries by Laidlaw and Kirkpatrick helped set up a dramatic 9-8 New Zealand win. The match was marred by a controversial decision by linesman Max Baise, who disallowed a Bryan Williams try but any thoughts of bias were dismissed when the All Blacks were awarded a 71st-minute penalty in front of the posts, which McCormick converted to end the day's scoring.

"We struggled to focus ourselves as we had for the first test," de Villiers says. "If you give the All Blacks any kind of advantage you can be sure they will take it and hammer it home. We made the mistake of dropping a few passes and missing a few kicks at goal. When you do that against New Zealand it is very rare that you end up on the winning side."

The resolve within the Springbok side for the third test in Port Elizabeth was strengthened with the news that Colin Meads would return to the All Black team. "You don't need any extra motivation when you play the All Blacks but the addition of Meads just helped us toughen our attitude. He was a truly great player. We all had a lot of respect for him but we were determined he wouldn't play a significant role in the series."

The Springboks' determination to win the test was unquestionable. Prop Mof Myburgh was brought into the team to counter the All Blacks' improving scrum while No 8 Lofty Nel was selected to help combat Lochore, Wyllie and Kirkpatrick.

"There was a real feeling of now or never," says de Villiers. "It was extremely disappointing to have lost at Newlands because we were now in a situation where, if we lost, we'd be down 1-2 despite the glory of the first test. It was time for us to stand up and be counted as a team.

"We were over the disappointment of the northern hemisphere tour. We'd grown as a team and we knew we were capable of peaking again. Yes, we were playing a good side, but we knew we couldn't worry about New Zealand. We had to make sure we did the things we wanted to do. Our destiny was in our hands and it was up to us to make it count for something."

As he did in the first test, de Villiers led from the front. With the Springboks leading by 6-3 in the second half, the halfback broke the game open with a burst down the All Black blindside before off-loading a pass to winger Gert Muller for the first of his two tries. The test was won 14-3 and the Springboks found themselves in an unbeatable position.

"Any real celebrations were put on hold," says de Villiers, "because we wanted to win the series. It wouldn't be good enough to draw the series. Maybe if some of us hadn't been on the 1965 tour, a drawn series with such a good All Black team may have been acceptable. But we were there. We wanted to give the All Blacks a taste of what it is like to lose a series. It was now as much about winning as it was seeing the All Blacks lose."

The disappointing display at Boet Erasmus Stadium caused Vodanovich to lose patience with a number of under-performing All Blacks. Long-standing international Earle Kirton was dropped from the test side as were winger Buff Milner and prop Neil Thimbleby. Chris Laidlaw was unavailable for selection after having his appendix removed. None of them wore the All Black test jersey again.

De Villiers had enjoyed a five-year rivalry with Laidlaw and while his replacement Sid Going would go on to become arguably New Zealand's best halfback, de Villiers' vote will always be with Laidlaw.

"Chris Laidlaw was as solid as a rock," he says. "He could serve a backline like few scrumhalves could. He had a long, quick, accurate pass whereas Sid Going was more flashy. He had a great burst of speed and used to love making quick breaks up the middle of the field. People remember Going more clearly because he was so dynamic. They don't remember the solid service of a player like Laidlaw. He rated highly in all categories except perhaps flamboyance. But that doesn't make Going a better player... it just makes him more popular."

Going's selection for the fourth test at Ellis Park offered much hope to the All Blacks' cause. When he had replaced the injured Laidlaw during the first test he had impressed with a number of darting runs. Blair Furlong was in the No 10 jersey and hopes were high the duo would be able to ignite the All Black backline.

But for that to happen the All Black forwards would have to at least gain parity – something they had failed to do in two of the first three tests. Jazz Muller was brought back into the front row after missing the third test and he was joined by Otago prop Keith Murdoch, who was given his debut cap.

"We knew the All Blacks would not lie down for us," says de Villiers. "We knew that we would have to beat them. Against some countries, when you have beaten them the week before, you know they are almost defeated before they take the field the following week. But against the All Blacks – an All Black team led by a man like Brian Lochore – you knew that they would be a tougher proposition the week after a loss.

"That's something the Springboks like to claim as well. The fame of rugby in both countries demands it. There are many similarities between rugby in New Zealand and rugby in South Africa. I think I know what it would be like to play against a Springbok side because the All Blacks had such similar attributes. We were all brought up on the traditions of rugby. If we didn't play rugby at school the sports master would want to know why.

"We are both the children of physical men – men who in South Africa worked in the mines and men who in New Zealand worked on the farms. We both enjoy the physical side of the game. The harder it is, the more we enjoy it. So yes, we knew the All Blacks would not hand us the series. It was going to be a real test of our resolve. It was judgment day again for all of us."

The Springboks would win the Ellis Park showdown 20-17. The All Blacks had fronted. Bryan Williams had scored a brilliant try and Gerald Kember stepped in for Fergie McCormick to slot home four penalties and a conversion. But this was South Africa's day. The shadows cast in 1965 were drawn back once and for all. The dream had been accomplished.

"This was, quite simply, brilliant," de Villiers says. "After the game I remember going into a dream world. It was too good to be true. *We've done it. We've beaten the All Blacks.* It was the ultimate."

The Ellis Park test signalled the end of a number of All Black careers. Grahame Thorne, Malcolm Dick and Ian MacRae announced their retirements while Blair Furlong and Gerald

Kember were never again in favour with the All Black selectors.

It was also the end of the road for de Villiers. After 22 tests as captain, this was his goodbye.

One of the reasons for his early retirement – he was only 30 at the time – was his disillusionment with the way the game was being covered in the republic. As captain of South Africa he had been the toast of the country after leading the Boks to series wins against Australia, France and New Zealand. But in 1965 he was singled out for special criticism after the series loss in New Zealand.

"People who read the newspapers forget after a year or two how much you were criticised," he says. "But these things... they do not just run off players. You feel the press. You feel the antagonism. You feel the criticism. One of the most difficult times in my life was returning home in 1965. The continuous analyses in newspapers of the tour on our return went on and on. They tore the team totally apart. Perhaps that is part of the medicine the sports editors thought the country needed before the recovery could start again. All I know is that it was not pleasant.

"There was no reason to keep playing," he says. "The All Blacks had come to Africa and we'd beaten them. That's as good as it gets."

DAWIE de VILLIERS AGAINST THE ALL BLACKS

Date	For	Venue	Result	Score	Points
31-7-65	South Africa	Wellington	lost	3-6	
4-9-65	South Africa	Christchurch	won	19-16	
18-9-65	South Africa	Auckland	lost	3-20	
11-7-70	Transvaal	Johannesburg	lost	17-34	try
25-7-70	South Africa	Pretoria	won	17-6	try
8-8-70	South Africa	Cape Town	lost	8-9	
29-8-70	South Africa	Port Elizabeth	won	14-3	
12-9-70	South Africa	Johannesburg	won	20-17	

TEST MATCH CAREER

	P	W	L	D	T	C	P	Dg	Pts
vs All Blacks	7	4	3	-	1	-	-	-	3
All Tests	25	15	6	4	3	-	-	-	9

Gareth Edwards

Date of birth: 12-7-1947
Born at: Gwaun-Cae-Gurwen,
　　　　　Wales
Position: Halfback
Test matches: 63

"Gareth Edwards was a tremendous player. He was a cocky sort of guy, a bit bigger than me, probably faster. The press always made a huge deal out of our rivalry. I had an enormous regard for Gareth"

Sid Going
(**Legends of the All Blacks,** 1999)

THERE are those of a certain age who don't just recall the exact sequence leading to Gareth Edwards' remarkable try for the Barbarians against the All Blacks at Cardiff Arms Park in 1973, they can actually repeat Cliff Morgan's evocative commentary verbatim: "Phil Bennett covering, chased by Alistair Scown. Brilliant, that's brilliant. John Williams... Pullin, John Dawes. Great dummy. David, Tom David, the halfway line. Brilliant by Quinnell. This is Gareth Edwards. A dramatic start. What a score!"

Five Welshmen and an Englishman combined to create the chance for Edwards to score what has gone down in rugby history as one of the truly great tries. And it was fitting the try that captured the hearts of Great Britain was scored by a man regarded as one of the best to ever play the game.

It doesn't matter where in the world the former Welsh halfback is, a week does not go by without somebody mentioning the try to him. While Edwards still enjoys bathing in the glory of that January day, his merriment has little to do with the sensational aspect of the score. Edwards' joy is born out of the fact that his try contributed to a win against the All Blacks.

"If the game had been played against anyone else, yes, I would have enjoyed scoring that try but it wouldn't have meant as much," says Edwards. "But, it happened against the All Blacks, in Cardiff. It was a magical moment because we'd beaten New Zealand. Okay, it wasn't a test match but we were playing the All Blacks and when you play New Zealand you aren't just playing against 15 players. You are taking on all of the traditions and mystique that surround them. It was a truly remarkable day."

Spend any time with Edwards and you are left with the impression that his respect for the black jersey is second to none. He uses words like *breathtaking, arousing, exciting, magnificent, stimulating, stirring and stunning.* Maybe it shouldn't surprise us... after all heroes have their own heroes too. But this is Gareth Edwards. A man who was to rugby what George Best was to soccer. A player who was head and shoulders above any other player of his generation. A quick-witted halfback with 250-degree vision.

While Edwards was growing up in Gwaun-Cae-Gurwen – a village of no more than 2000 people 11 miles from Neath – the legend of the All Blacks was inescapable. Gwaun-Cae-Gurwen's most famous son in the early years of Edwards' life was the great Welsh centre of the 1930s, Claude Davey, who captained Wales to a 13-12 victory against New Zealand in 1935.

"He was the toast of the village," says Edwards. "An absolute legend. I was always being reminded about the great Welsh side that he captained as well as the great All Black team that he defeated. When the villagers talked about the All Blacks it was always dramatic.

"You have to remember that in those days there was no television. It's not like it is today where you can be in your living room and at the switch of a button you can watch Auckland play

Wellington on the other side of the world. So my knowledge of the All Blacks grew from listening to the villagers chat about the All Black touring teams they'd seen. I'd hear about these giants, men who were fearless, men who were in every way as tough as nails. Because the All Blacks toured only once a decade they had a great mystique about them. That's probably been lost a bit these days because tours happen much more frequently. We have the World Cup and there are a lot more opportunities for one-off games. I'm not saying today's tests between New Zealand and Wales have lost anything because the will to win would be as strong. But today's Welsh players have the advantage of videotape and satellites to study the way the All Blacks play. There are very few secrets nowadays.

"But when I was growing up, you really did believe these men were 10 feet tall. To play them for the first time was an immense thrill. It was something I'd grown up dreaming about. I had a huge respect for them and subsequently had a real determination to beat them because I was very much aware of what it meant to beat the All Blacks."

Edwards' first opportunity came at the age of 19, when he was included in the Welsh team for the 1967 test against Brian Lochore's All Blacks at Cardiff Arms Park – a match which doubled for the home side as a chance to avenge the whitewashing handed the Welsh-dominated 1966 Lions. Recent history may have been against them, but overall the record book was in Wales' favour – in the five tests between the two countries since the first in 1905, they had beaten New Zealand more times than they'd lost. And even though this time they were without their injured goalkicker Keith Jarrett it was widely believed they had a chance to add to their tally of three victories.

"The build-up to a game against New Zealand is different to any other. Opportunities to test yourself against them were quite rare. When you play an England or a France side you know that, if things go wrong one year, you'll have the opportunity to put things right the following season. But when you played the All Blacks there was a real feeling that you were playing for your place in history. This time people weren't only going to be talking about Claude Davey in the village. I knew there would be a few whispers about me and I wanted to make a good impression. I remember being filled with tremendous expectation and a certain amount of trepidation going into the game."

The All Blacks, playing with a strong wind in the first half, dominated the early phases of the test with a try by Waikato winger Bill Birtwistle securing them an 8-0 halftime lead. When the teams turned and Wales had the benefit of the wind it was expected the home team would have too much firepower. It could still be argued the Welsh had the better of the final 40 minutes but Wales' cause wasn't helped by a trio of missed penalty attempts, two by fullback Paul Wheeler and one by Edwards. When a dubious over-the-shoulder pass from No 8 John Jeffery was intercepted by Bill Davis, allowing him to score the All Blacks' second try, the game was beyond Wales' grasp, eventually to be won 13-6 by New Zealand... and Jeffery would never wear the Welsh jersey again.

"The harsh reality of playing against the All Blacks is that if you make mistakes the New Zealanders have a habit of winning games that perhaps they shouldn't," says Edwards. "I'm not suggesting we deserved to win the game but we had our opportunities and we didn't take them. While we were missing three second-half kicks within the space of 10 minutes, Fergie McCormick was taking the goalkicking chances he was presented with and, in the end, that was the difference.

"Winning test matches isn't always about the things you do, sometimes it comes down to the things you don't do. That was certainly the case on that day."

Later in the tour, and again at Cardiff Arms Park, Edwards had another chance against the All Blacks, this time for East Wales. And despite his youth, he was handed the captaincy.

Edwards recalls an incident from early in the game. He'd hoofed a huge up-and-under and as he was following it at a rate of knots he realised the ball was headed for the All Black centre Ian MacRae. Edwards knew that to have any chance of tackling the Hawke's Bay player he'd have to hit him hard. As he went in for the tackle there was an accidental clash of heads. "As I got up off the ground I caught a glimpse of the corner of his eye and blood was seeping from it. I remember looking at him and thinking *Good God, they do bleed!* I know it sounds a little silly now looking back but it was part and parcel of our upbringing... All Blacks didn't bleed."

Edwards was only minutes away from having his rivalry against New Zealand sweetened with a win but a late Tony Steel try secured a 3-3 draw. It was the second of three games against the All Blacks for Edwards that winter and the second of three heartbreaking results.

"It didn't take me very long to come to terms with how difficult it was going to be to beat the All Blacks," he says. "It's difficult to explain, but I don't know if they knew how to lose. Of course they lost the odd match, but it seemed like the losses only came when their opponents took every opportunity that came their way."

If Edwards was thirsting for opportunities to match himself against the All Blacks, he didn't have long to wait. Heavy snowfalls had caused the East Wales match to be postponed from its original Saturday date to the following Wednesday and just three days later he was given another chance at redemption. With the All Blacks' game against Ireland called off because of an outbreak of foot and mouth disease, a Barbarians match at Twickenham was organised and Edwards joined five Welshmen, six Englishmen and three Scots for his third attempt at beating New Zealand that winter.

As with the East Wales game, Edwards was convinced this match would be won when, with less than five minutes to go, the Baabaas led by 6-3. But when a midfield break by Steel was only partially halted, the winger managed to slip the ball to MacRae, who ran on to score. Then, with the game all but over and seemingly headed for a draw, Lochore latched on to a misplaced kick from Scottish fullback Stewart Wilson and started a move which ended with Steel scoring, McCormick converting and the New Zealanders 11-6 winners.

"The All Blacks were accustomed to winning and regardless of how ordinary they may have played at times, they always seemed to sneak a result, Edwards says. "Unfortunately, it was a lesson that I would be reminded of a few more times as my career continued."

‹♣›

REPUTATIONS count for little once a test match starts. The old adage of *you are only as good as your last game* will continue to ring true just as it did when the 1969 Welsh team arrived in New Zealand.

If reputations did count for anything, the Welsh would have at least matched Brian Lochore's All Blacks in the two-test series. But despite the Welsh arriving in New Zealand as both Triple Crown winners and Five Nations champions – and boasting a backline that was second to none in world rugby with names like Gareth Edwards, Barry John, Gerald Davies and JPR Williams – the series was lost 2-0.

Edwards, who tweaked a hamstring in the build-up to the first test, had a quiet match as Wales went down 19-0. "The injury wasn't a factor because I never really got my hands on the ball. It was like there were a hundred All Blacks out there. It was very much a case of black wave after black wave of pressure. There we were, playing the All Blacks on their own patch, being taken apart limb by limb. It was a comprehensive win to the All Blacks but even the scoreline of 19-0 didn't show what a poor second we were."

The Welsh weren't helped by an itinerary that most teams would have struggled with. They arrived in New Zealand only eight days prior to the first test at Lancaster Park. That's probably four or five days longer than today's players enjoy but in 1969 New Zealand was more than just a 20 hour flight away from Cardiff. The flight to New Zealand included 48 hours of actual flying time and nine stopovers.

With wins recorded against Otago and Wellington, and the team having more time to adjust to their new surroundings, a better Welsh effort was expected in the second test at Eden Park. But while Wales was able to finally break the All Black defence and score two tries, they were well beaten at 33-12, with McCormick in inspirational form scoring a world record 24 points.

While some sections of the New Zealand media were content to just celebrate the All Black series win, others took joy in printing stinging attacks on the Welsh. "By the end of the series it was obvious that the New Zealand media and public had very little respect for us. I think they thought we were living off our reputations a little bit. But I don't know that we were arrogant. We were just confident. We'd had a lot of success in Europe and while we knew playing the All Blacks away from home would be a step up, there was still a belief that we could win. It wasn't easy being so heavily criticised but if you don't learn from your mistakes it is a missed opportunity.

"What the criticism did do was serve its purpose for the nucleus of the Lions team that would return to New Zealand two years later. Unless you have toured New Zealand you can't begin to understand how difficult it is. But even though we'd lost we could take comfort from the fact that we'd gone there, we'd touched it, we'd felt it. We knew the environment and we could prepare ourselves for the intensity. The greatest lesson we learned was that it didn't matter how good you thought you were or how well you thought you prepared, to beat New Zealand you have got to be even better.

"I don't think the success of the Lions in 1971 was a coincidence because the criticism the 1969 side received gave the Welsh contingent of the Lions team a defiant determination to prove that we could play good rugby."

When Edwards returned for the Lions tour he had developed into one of the superstars of rugby. His combination with first-five Barry John was the most feared inside back combination at the time. Edwards' ability to accurately pass the ball substantial distances allowed John the freedom to roam outside the normal jurisdiction of a first-five. It was a combination that their New Zealand counterparts, Sid Going and Bob Burgess, struggled to contain throughout the four-test series.

The first test in Dunedin was won by the Lions 9-3 and despite the All Blacks levelling the series with a 22-12 win in the second test at Lancaster Park the confidence within the British side never wavered.

"We knew the All Blacks would come out firing in the second test," says Edwards. "They would have been furious at losing in Dunedin because for the first 15 minutes they absolutely dominated us. How they didn't score three or four tries I'll never know. Our defence was superb. There was a real determination not to let them cross our line. I think all the players in the side had learned from their previous experiences against the All Blacks. The All Blacks always had a steely edge to their defence and it was something that we'd adopted.

"In the second test, we didn't play well but even though they scored five tries against us we hadn't been that impressed with the performance of the All Blacks either. I don't want to detract from New Zealand's performance that day but our attitude was that if that was the best New Zealand could play, we were good enough to win the series. It was a strange scene in the dressing room because we were all sitting there convinced we'd be good enough to be the first Lions side to win in New Zealand. There was a strong feeling of confidence... not the sort of reaction you would normally expect from a team that had just been beaten by 10 points."

A big part of the reason for the side's confidence came from their former Welsh international coach Carwyn James. "He was a great motivator – one of those guys who could really make you believe that you could do what he wanted you to do. For once we believed we were better than New Zealand. Man-for-man we were as good as if not better than them. Every side will tell you that's what they happen to think, but we really believed it. In 1969 we said we were as good as the All Blacks, but I'm not so sure we believed it to a man."

Edwards was inspirational in the third test at Athletic Park as the Lions recaptured control of the series and when JPR Williams' dropped goal in the fourth test at Eden Park secured a 14-14 draw, the 1971 Lions had made history.

As New Zealand was thrown into the depths of rugby darkness, Delme Thomas, JPR Williams, Mervyn Davies, Barry John, Gerald Davies, John Dawes, John Taylor and Edwards had indeed returned from the 1969 tour to prove once and for all that Wales deserved the reputation it had for producing world-class players. The United Kingdom was in raptures – for the first time, a Lions team had won a series in New Zealand.

"When I came back from my first Lions tour [a series loss to South Africa in 1968] everyone in Gwaun-Cae-Gurwen knew I'd been away but nobody made a fuss about me when I got home. I'd be walking down the road and all I'd get would be a 'How are you?' Well... when I got home from New Zealand it was really quite unbelievable. Tens of thousands of people met the team when we arrived at Heathrow. At the time they said it was the biggest crowd at the airport since the Beatles returned from America in the mid-sixties. Bus loads of people had come from all over the country to pay tribute to what we'd achieved.

"We stayed overnight in London and the following day I jumped on the train to go home to Wales with my girlfriend. For the entire two-and-a-half-hour journey different people were coming up to me and offering their congratulations.

"When we got to Neath, the platform was overflowing with people. The Lord Mayor was there, there were flowers for my mother and flowers for my grandmother. As we walked out through the masses of people we got into some vintage cars that drove us to the village. It was the longest 11 miles of my life! You literally couldn't move. It was as though a carnival had come to town. There were kids lined up for miles, people were waving flags, people were cheering, people were singing. When we got to Gwaun-Cae-Gurwen I was taken straight to the village hall which was overflowing with two thousand people. There were more speeches, more welcomes, more well-dones, more bands, more television, more this and more that. It was very special.

"If I needed a reminder, that was the difference between winning in New Zealand and losing in South Africa. The celebrations were born out of the tremendous respect every Welshman has for the All Blacks. It wasn't simply a case of celebrating a Lions' victory, it was about beating the All Blacks... In a way, that outpouring from the people of Wales was the biggest sign they could give to the way they felt about the traditions of the mighty All Blacks."

ॐ

NEVER underestimate the heart of an All Black. It was a lesson Edwards learned from listening to the local villagers as a child and from his experiences against them on the rugby field. But it would take one more test against the New Zealanders to finally make the lesson stick.

When Ian Kirkpatrick's All Blacks arrived for a five-test tour of the British Isles and France in 1972 it was widely accepted that if the New Zealanders' hopes of a Grand Slam were to come unstuck, the most obvious prediction for a defeat would be in the first of the tests, against Wales at Cardiff Arms Park.

Despite the All Blacks' whitewashing of the Australians 3-0 in a home series before heading to the United Kingdom, Kirkpatrick's side had an unextraordinary look about it. After the series loss against the Lions the previous year, the All Blacks had lost the services of Colin Meads, Wayne Cottrell, Jazz Muller and Tom Lister. Seven players were given debuts for the first test of the year against the Wallabies but out of that list of fullback Trevor Morris, winger Duncan Hales, centre Bruce Robertson, second five Mike Parkinson, flanker Alistair Scown and props Graham Whiting and Jeff Matheson, only Robertson would go on to have a prominent All Black career.

"While that All Black team had great players like Ian Kirkpatrick, Tane Norton, Alex Wyllie, Sid Going and Bryan Williams, there was a fragile look about the side," Edwards says. "It certainly wasn't the best All Black team sent away to tour Britain. At other times when I'd played New Zealand it was a case of admitting to ourselves that, okay, the New Zealand side was better. But not on this occasion. On paper – and a test has never been won on paper as far as I know – we were a much more experienced and skilled team. But, and maybe we should have seen it coming, when New Zealanders pull on that black jersey something happens to them. It's as if they grow another heart. If some of the side were boys when they left New Zealand, they were men by the time they ran onto the Arms Park in the All Black strip."

The test, which would be Edwards' last against New Zealand, rates as the biggest disappointment in his remarkable career. Going into the test, the All Blacks had already suffered two losses – to Llanelli 3-9 and 14-16 to a Northern-Western Counties selection. And while the All Black scrum were struggling to manage without Meads in the engine room, the Welsh were in the encouraging position of being able to select JPR Williams, Gerald Davies, John Bevan, Mervyn Davies, John Taylor, Delme Thomas and Derek Quinnell, who were still riding the high of the victorious Lions tour.

But it was the All Blacks, with their much-criticised pack leading the way by winning three tight-heads, who would emerge with the 19-

16 scoreline in their favour. As had happened in the 1967 test at the same ground, the Welsh were let down by some poor goalkicking. While Joe Karam was in magnificent form slotting five penalty goals, Welsh first-five Phil Bennett, who had taken over from the now-retired Barry John, was locked in a mediocre performance, missing three shots at goal including a late penalty that would have drawn the game.

The Welsh were heartbroken, in particular Edwards who had once again been the standout performer for the home side.

"When you get your opportunities in test matches, you have to take them. Historically the All Blacks have proven that. It doesn't matter if it's a one-sided game or a close game, the All Blacks always seem to be able to adapt. That's what makes New Zealand so difficult to beat; they take their chances no matter what the circumstances are. Obviously there is an element of how well the opposition let them play. With the Lions, we were able to limit their opportunities. That's the key. You can't give them a sniff, because if you do they won't only put another nail in the coffin, they'll bury you as well."

While Keith Murdoch was the toast of the All Blacks after scoring New Zealand's game-breaking try, Edwards finds it difficult not to heap praise on his opposite, Sid Going. The All Black halfback laid on the pass for Murdoch's score and his darting runs from the base of the New Zealand scrum caused on-going problems for Edwards and the Welsh loose forwards David Morris, Mervyn Davies and John Taylor.

"It was a typical performance from Sid," says Edwards, who played 53 tests for Wales and 10 for the Lions. "Of all the halfbacks I played against he was the one who gave me the most trouble. In fact, on more than one occasion he got the better of me, no question about that.

"In 1967 when I played against New Zealand it was Chris Laidlaw behind the All Black scrum. He was a lovely reader of the game and he was also an extremely good passer but Sid was by far the more aggressive and dangerous player. He was like a terrier. You really had to keep an eye on him all of the time. It didn't help that in most of the matches that I played against him it was the New Zealand pack that had the ascendancy.

"And I think I am qualified to say that there is nothing an All Black loose forward likes better than going after little halfbacks. Unfortunately, whenever I played against Sid in tests, I had some of the great names of All Black rugby – men like Ian Kirkpatrick, Brian Lochore, Alan Sutherland and Alex Wyllie – hunting me down."

One of the few times a British side got the better of Going was in the third Lions test in 1971. Says Edwards: "Derek Quinnell, who hadn't even played for Wales at that time, was selected for the Lions team and given the responsibility of stopping Super Sid. Derek spent the week practising his tackling and in the test match Sid was virtually eliminated. We encouraged Sid to look for space on the blindside where Quinnell was lying in wait and he fell for our trap. That was one of the main reasons why we won that vital test."

While Quinnell stood up to be counted on that occasion it is worth contemplating the frustration Edwards would have felt when players around him failed. Edwards wasn't the perfect footballer but he was one of the most talented. His heroics in New Zealand in 1971 and in South Africa for the Lions in 1974, when they beat the Springboks 3-0, were in a class of their own. He was arguably the greatest athlete to have graced a rugby field. Once when asked on the eve of an international to undergo a fitness test, Edwards looked the chairman of selectors in the eye, smiled, and then proceeded to do 20 back somersaults on the spot. The fitness test was cancelled.

So, while he's not complaining, you can understand the burden of playing out a career with some players nowhere near his high standards. Edwards learned to deal with it, in part, by watching the way some of the great All Blacks coped with a similar scenario.

"Men like Brian Lochore, Colin Meads and Ian Kirkpatrick were obviously classy players but while some of the players who played with them couldn't be classed as great, the thing the great players did was make the others around them better.

"An ultimate side is a team that has no weaknesses and no side can ever claim that. The All Blacks were always very good at acknowledging their weak points and coming up with ways of compensating. The All Blacks proved in 1972 that just because the opposition has better players doesn't mean they are automatically the better team. It's possible that we could have won or at least drawn that game if Barry John had been playing instead of Phil Bennett. And it's possible that Wales would have beaten the 1967 All Blacks if John Jeffery hadn't made that errant pass. But I would never criticise either of those players. They gave their all in those games and I would never blame an individual player for a loss.

"Just because you are one of the better or more senior players in the team doesn't give you the right to do that. If you are lucky enough to be in either category, then the only responsibility that gives you is to try and make the players around you better. It's something the great All Blacks have been doing for generations."

❧

THERE can be no argument. It was simply the best rugby game ever played. When Ian Kirkpatrick's All Black side headed to Wales for the clash against the Barbarians, the anticipation level was rightly high. The New Zealanders, coming to the end of a tour where they had remained undefeated in tests against Wales, Scotland, England and Ireland, had proven the critics wrong and matured into a good All Black team. And the Barbarians, stacked with the stars of the 1971 Lions tour, were determined to once again prove they could overcome the legend of the All Blacks.

Games with such high expectations rarely live up to the hype but this was the exception. Any poll of the millennium's top tries would have to include two from Cardiff Arms Park that day – Edwards' effort early in the game and JPR Williams' decisive second-half try. The All Blacks added to the occasion as well with some spectacular play from winger Grant Batty, although he couldn't prevent the All Blacks going down 11-23.

Ironically, despite the tradition of the Barbarians calling for an open attacking game, pressure from the British fans convinced the players to rate winning as a higher priority than entertaining.

"Normally, Barbarian matches are all about just going out there and having a go," says Edwards. "But even though we were wearing the Barbarian jersey, that game wasn't the time or place for throwing the ball about. As it happened, once the lads had combined to set me up for the early try, the game developed into one of the most entertaining games of rugby ever played, but that certainly wasn't the plan."

After the disappointments of tests against the All Blacks that winter – Wales lost 19-16, Scotland were defeated 14-9, England faded to a 9-0 loss and Ireland were held to a 10-10 draw – the British media and fans were desperate for some success. It was also the first opportunity they had to see the nucleus of the 1971 Lions team reunited to do battle against the old foe.

"We didn't want to let the people down," says Edwards. "A lot of the people crammed into the park that day were the same people who sent us telegrams and letters during the Lions tour. There was tremendous pressure on us because we knew they were expecting us to play the way we did when we were in New Zealand. But the fact was that we weren't on tour. We'd only come together two days before the game and obviously we hadn't had the opportunity to play with each other in the meantime. The training session that we had was the worst one that I ever attended in my career. The combinations weren't there, there were dropped passes and lots of other mistakes. And then prior to the game Gerald Davies pulled out after injuring a hamstring and Mervyn Davies got influenza. As it turned out, both of their replacements – Tom David and Derek Quinnell – played a part in our first try.

"My try took a little bit of pressure off us and we became prepared to play an open style of rugby and in the first half it paid off. Quite honestly I could not believe we led 17-0 at halftime. The amazing thing was that it could have been more. We'd taken New Zealand by surprise but we knew they'd come back at us.

"At halftime we all went into a huddle and I could sense a nervousness from some of the lads. I think we all knew what was coming. You don't put 17 points on the All Blacks and expect them to lay over and die. We knew they'd come at us with all guns blazing. Willie John McBride, the great Irish lock, said, 'We might have played well, but the game starts now.' Sure enough, the All Blacks came out like men possessed. It didn't matter how much you prepared for an All Black onslaught... once it came you just had to find a way to ride through it and wait for an opportunity to relieve the pressure. For the first 25 minutes of the second half they had us on the ropes.

"The thing that helped us eventually hold on to win was that the majority of our players knew what it took to beat the All Blacks. We knew about the desperate defending. We knew we had to put our bodies on the line. If we hadn't already lived through what you have to do to beat the All Blacks, there would have been no way we would have coped with the onslaught."

The Barbarians' victory dominated rugby headlines in the UK for days. And while the result wasn't as significant as the Lions' series win or any other win against the All Blacks, it was celebrated as though it was. "The victory meant everything to the team and their supporters but not just because of the type of game we played," says Edwards. "The joy was there because the win had come against the All Blacks. The biggest compliment I could ever give the All Blacks is that the win meant everything to us."

GARETH EDWARDS AGAINST THE ALL BLACKS

Date	For	Venue	Result	Score	Points
11-11-67	Wales	Cardiff	lost	6-13	
13-12-67	East Wales	Cardiff	drew	3-3	
16-12-67	Barbarians	London	lost	6-11	
31-5-69	Wales	Christchurch	lost	0-19	
14-6-69	Wales	Auckland	lost	12-33	
26-6-71	British Isles	Dunedin	won	9-3	
10-7-71	British Isles	Christchurch	lost	12-22	
31-7-71	British Isles	Wellington	won	13-3	
14-8-71	British Isles	Auckland	drew	14-14	
4-11-72	Cardiff	Cardiff	lost	4-20	try
2-12-72	Wales	Cardiff	lost	16-19	
27-1-73	Barbarians	Cardiff	won	23-11	try
27-11-74	Welsh XV	Cardiff	lost	3-12	
30-11-74	Barbarians	London	drew	13-13	

TEST MATCH CAREER

	P	W	L	D	T	C	P	Dg	Pts
vs All Blacks	8	2	5	1	-	-	-	-	-
All Tests	63	39	16	8	20	2	3	-	85

Gavin Hastings

Date of birth: 3-1-1962
Born at: Edinburgh, Scotland
Position: Fullback
Test matches: 67

"Gavin benefited greatly from the time he spent playing club rugby in New Zealand. I'm sure it played a big part in him eventually maturing into one of the great footballers. He was the rock within the Scotland team – one of those rare breeds of players capable of playing mistake-free rugby"

John Gallagher

WHILE standing on the doorstep of history, contemplating the battle ahead and thinking of his side's possible place in Lions' folklore, his mood was ambushed. Gavin Hastings had only minutes before he emerged from underneath the Eden Park grandstand after delivering a stirring team-talk. Throughout the tour the Lions' captain had stressed the importance of total concentration and this day was no different.

He had talked of the importance of never letting your guard down against the mighty All Blacks. So the scene was set. The series was locked at one test apiece and all the signs suggested the decider would be a thriller. Hastings led his team onto the park and after the national anthems lined up to face the All Black haka.

He had been here before. There had been eight previous occasions when he had accepted the famous Maori challenge. He was an old hand at it – pick out an All Black, look him in the eye and stand your ground. The player he found himself confronting was Va'aiga Tuigamala...

"Of all the All Blacks I saw perform the haka, Inga was the most expressive. He was always totally into it. His eyes looked like they were going to pop out of his head and his facial expression and the power that he thumped the ground with was always impressive. I lined myself up with him and when the haka began we eyeballed each other. I was up for it. I had a bit of a scowl on my face and I was thinking to myself that I couldn't wait for the game to start so I could have a go at him. It was very intense. Anyone who wasn't convinced the occasion was an important one only needed to have seen the All Black haka that day.

"As the haka was coming to a close you could sense that Inga's blood was boiling. Mine was as well. I was ready for action when, just as Inga had finished his leap into the air at the end of it, he winked at me and flashed a great big smile my way! It was one of those priceless moments you never forget.

"To me it summed up All Black rugby. Sometimes the Blacks are talked about as being humourless giants with nothing on their minds but winning. That desire to win is always there but make no mistake about it... there are plenty of characters in New Zealand rugby."

It's true that Tuigamala was one of New Zealand rugby's great characters in 1993 but the winger's gesture to Hastings that July day was born out of something much deeper than character. For Tuigamala it was a way of paying respect to a player who only a week earlier had been responsible for the demise of the All Blacks.

ða

HASTINGS' first All Black experience came during the 1987 World Cup. Scotland had become New Zealand's quarter-final opponents by virtue of finishing second to France in their pool. Leading into the test at Christchurch, Scotland had drawn with the French before going on to defeat Zimbabwe and Romania. The strength of the Scottish side was built around a forward eight led by the power-packed hooker and captain Colin Deans. Scotland had never beaten the All Blacks, although four years earlier Hastings had watched Scotland fight to a 25-all draw at Murrayfield. Deans, fellow front-rower Ian Milne, No 8 Iain Paxton and halfback Roy Laidlaw were backing up from that test as Hastings prepared for the game he'd waited a lifetime to play.

"Before you play the All Blacks for the first time there is always this great myth about them. They are the most feared team in rugby; so much so that the fear of losing to them can consume a team. Colin Deans was a very inspirational captain and he spent a lot of time talking to the younger players in the team, trying to convince us that the All Blacks were beatable. But it was a daunting task. It didn't matter what anyone said, playing the All Blacks was going to be a severe test.

"There is no question the first time you face up to the haka – not knowing what to expect, not knowing how it is going to affect you – is intimidating. By the end of my career I was a firm believer that the All Blacks probably have an advantage going into a game because of the myth that surrounds them. If you play rugby at any level anywhere around the world, there is a good chance that you will know something of the All Blacks. You are forever hearing about the great All Black sides of the past and when you actually go to New Zealand it's difficult not to be impressed by the pride and the passion that New Zealanders have for their team.

"It's ironic that Colin Deans spent so much time trying to get me to believe that we could win the quarter-final because it would be only three years later that I was the captain and forever trying to convince people that these were not superhuman beings that we were facing up to.

"When there are enough of you in a team who have played against the All Blacks, obviously your chances of victory get very much greater. There have been two or three times in my career when I've come off the field against them and looked at my teammates and thought that we really should have won that game. Perhaps if we'd carried a little bit more conviction into the game with them, then the result might have been different.

"Deans' inspiration was lost on the Scotland side that day,

though, as we were thumped 30-3. He was convinced the 1987 team were capable of being beaten... in fact, that year they weren't. They were so far ahead of all the other teams competing at the World Cup.

"The All Black forwards didn't give us a look in. The front row of John Drake, Sean Fitzpatrick and Steve McDowell were the best in the world and in Michael Jones they had a player who, even then, you could tell was destined for greatness. And the backs... they were lethal. No one could have stopped them. David Kirk was a good halfback and Grant Fox was the master technician at first five-eighth.

"It's interesting that so many people choose only to remember Foxy for his kicking ability. His distribution to his outsides was first class. I have no doubt the backline wouldn't have operated anywhere near as productively as it did if Foxy hadn't been there. I'm sure that John Gallagher, John Kirwan and Craig Green appreciated him, even if some New Zealanders didn't."

Hastings was an instant fan of New Zealand rugby. He had impressed during the World Cup with his heroics in the Scottish backline and his wanting to test himself against the best fuelled his desire to remain in New Zealand long after the All Blacks had defeated France in a one-sided final. He relocated himself to Auckland and joined the University club. During a season where he helped Varsity prevail in Auckland's Gallaher Shield he was given a unique insight into two of the personalities who would dominate New Zealand rugby for years to come. Fox and Fitzpatrick were two of his new teammates.

"It was the biggest learning curve I'd been on. The thing that struck me the most about them was their total professionalism. It was extraordinary. Even something as simple as their attitude in training influenced me for the rest of my career. The attitude to training back home was always that it was a bit of a laugh – a place for the lads to get together, run a few moves and take the mickey out of someone if they dropped the ball. Foxy was so professional that if one of us dropped the ball he wanted to know why! Was it a bad pass? A lack of concentration? That was to my mind the one thing the All Blacks did better than anyone. They trained the way they wanted to play a game."

Hastings was also given an early sighting of the feisty attitude that Fitzpatrick would make famous over the next nine years as he completed an All Black career that saw him play a New Zealand record 92 tests and finish the millennium as runner-up to the great Colin Meads in a Player of the Century poll. The incident happened in Japan during the All Blacks' 1987 post-World Cup tour. Hastings was playing for one of the Japanese invitational sides...

"I was looking forward to the game because I'd got to know a few of the All Blacks and I thought it might be a fun occasion. In the first minute of the game I got myself underneath an up-and-under and within seconds I found myself at the bottom of an All Black ruck when someone gave me a good kick up the arse. I looked up and it was Fitzy. I realised the field was the place where friendship ends. After the game he shook my hand and we shared a beer at the bar. For me, he was the consummate professional. Off the field he was one of the nicest blokes around... on the field he was as tough as they come and he always used his talents to the limits. There were a few times when Fitzy left the field after taking a hammering from opposing players who took out their frustration on him but Fitzy would never complain. He'd just smile and say *Live by the sword, die by the sword*."

Hastings took the lessons from his New Zealand experience back to Scotland and implemented them into the Scottish set-up. He fronted for trainings with the desire to train as he intended to play. When balls were dropped or when players lagged behind in training runs there was no more laughter. Stern encouragement was offered and his teammates responded. The new mood coupled with the natural maturing of the team that played the All Blacks in 1987 meant that, by the time Hastings returned to New Zealand for the Scottish tour in 1990, they were Five Nations champions by virtue of a Grand Slam.

The All Blacks went into the two-test series unbeaten in their previous 13 international outings. And despite the Scots being spearheaded by six players who had played in the World Cup quarter-final – Iwan Tukalo, Finlay Calder, Derek White, Hastings and captain David Sole – few gave them a chance of upsetting Alex Wyllie's team, which was at full strength.

The first test at Carisbrook was a one-sided affair. Kirwan, playing his first test since snapping his Achilles tendon the year before in Wales, scored two of the All Blacks' five tries as they cruised to a 31-16 victory. Hastings and Sole were standout players for the Scots but as the teams prepared for the second test in Auckland everyone except for Ian McGeechan's men expected a whitewash.

"We were well beaten but we felt as though we'd let in two or three soft scores," says Hastings. "I thought that we had been more inventive in the backs than the All Blacks so I certainly thought that if we got our act together we might have a chance. No one likes to get beaten the way we did in Dunedin and there was a real determination to prove to everyone that we belonged on the same field as the All Blacks.

"There was never any complacency about the task that was ahead of us when we arrived in New Zealand but the fact that we'd recently won the Grand Slam may have taken the edge off us a little bit. Ian McGeechan was desperate for us to put in a better effort in the second test and he reminded us that if we wanted respect from New Zealanders, the only place we were going to earn it was on the field."

Hastings doesn't look back on the game with too much comfort. After the Scots led 18-12 at halftime the All Blacks slowly took control. Despite the best efforts of the impressive Scottish loosies Calder and John Jeffrey, the All Black pack began to dominate and after an early second-half penalty by Fox closed the gap to three points, Hastings found himself at the centre of a controversy. With 15 minutes to go, standing in his 22, he fielded a punt from All Black fullback Kieran Crowley and headed infield. He was tackled by Mike Brewer, who appeared to be within the 10-metre circle, and was penalised by Welsh referee Derek Bevan for not releasing the ball. Fox landed the penalty and five minutes later another penalty from the Auckland kicker sealed the 21-18 win.

"I still feel uneasy when I look back at that game. There was no way a penalty should have been awarded against me. No way. It is not often in a player's career when you have a chance to beat the All Blacks and for it to be snatched away from you by a referee doesn't sit well with me. A victory against the Blacks is such a rare thing... I guess that's why it still upsets me a bit. If the same incident had happened against Wales or England it would still hurt but when you play in the Five Nations you always have the knowledge that you'll have a chance at redemption every year. I'm sure that's one of the reasons wins against the All Blacks are so precious."

When Hastings and his teammates arrived back in Scotland news filtered through from New Zealand that Wayne Shelford had been dumped from the All Blacks after an indifferent series. While the majority of New Zealanders couldn't understand the decision to hand the captaincy to Gary Whetton, Hastings was one of the few who wasn't surprised.

"I must admit that I wasn't too impressed with Buck during the series. I thought he was living off his reputation a bit. There was no question that in his day he was a great player but by the time we toured he was well past his best. I know his axing didn't go down too well in New Zealand but in hindsight it probably didn't do him any harm because it played a major part in him assuming the legendary status he now enjoys."

⁊⁊

ALL the signs pointed to Gavin Hastings' epitaph reading *Cause of death... All Blacks*. For all his talent, Hastings seemed destined never to be on a winning team against New Zealand. The loss in 1987 and double test defeats in 1990 were followed by a 13-6 loss in the third and fourth places play-off at the 1991 World Cup. Adding to his uncertainty was the depletion of the Scotland side. By the time Scotland hosted New Zealand in 1993, seven of the forward pack from the World Cup battle had retired or been retired by Scotland's selectors while the backs were missing their influential halfback Gary Armstrong and centre Sean Lineen. The test was lost by an embarrassing scoreline of 51-15.

"For some unknown reason they played Scott [Gavin's brother] on the left wing. He was a centre but the selectors thought he'd go all right against Jeff Wilson! Goldie scored three tries and proved the Scottish selectors were absolutely naive."

While Scottish rugby was going through a rebuilding phase it was obvious to Hastings the elusive win against the All Blacks wouldn't come when he was wearing the famous dark blue strip. He was convinced his best opportunity would come in 1993 when the Lions were due to tour. But a year earlier there was an unexpected invitation and, from the All Black perspective, an even more unexpected victory.

Hastings' name was one of the first on the list as the New Zealand Rugby Union went about selecting a World XV to play three tests as part of its centenary celebrations. The first test was in Christchurch and even though it was the first test of Laurie Mains' All Black coaching reign, his side was still expected to be too strong for an opposing team that had assembled randomly with only a few days' preparation time.

But if there was a warning sign for Mains it was that the World XV squad included a core of players who knew what it took to beat the All Blacks. The Australian team that had beaten the All Blacks in the semifinal of the previous year's World Cup included Tim Horan, Willie Ofahengaue, John Eales, Nick Farr-Jones, Ewen McKenzie and Phil Kearns. "That was a real key for us," says Hastings. "When you are surrounded by guys who have been there and done it before, it's a whole lot easier to believe that success is possible."

The All Black debutants that day included Frank Bunce, Richard Turner, Arran Pene and Mark Cooksley but any celebrations they may have planned ended in misery as the World XV outclassed the All Blacks 28-14, the winning total the second-highest score ever posted against the All Blacks to that time.

While Mains was able to guide the All Blacks to a series win – winning the second test 54-26 and the third 26-15 – Hastings was basking in the knowledge that the breakthrough had been made.

"I'd been on a team that had defeated the mighty All Blacks. Okay, it wasn't a test where I was wearing the Scotland jersey or the Lions jersey, but it was a win. The fact that it came while playing for the World XV was good enough for me. Any win against the All Blacks is a great win – especially as the memories of 1990 were still fresh."

It is ironic then that just as Hastings had seemed to lay to rest the demons of 1990 he would return a year later for what would turn out to be the biggest disappointment of his career – thanks to an improved All Black team and an Australian referee by the name of Brian Kinsey.

It was no surprise when Hastings was named captain of the 1993 Lions. Considering that 16 of the 30-strong touring party were English, it goes a long way to explain the standing Hastings enjoyed in the UK for McGeechan to feel confident that his former Scotland charge would be accepted so readily by his new teammates.

The Lions arrived with high hopes. Despite New Zealand winning their last two tests of 1992, against Australia and South Africa, there were enough signs to suggest the All Blacks weren't the force they once were. Their win against Australia in Sydney came after consecutive loses to the Wallabies – the first series loss to the Australians since 1986.

The All Blacks went into the Lions series "cold". There were no matches against the likes of Argentina or Manu Samoa before the first test in Christchurch offering New Zealand a chance for a couple of blow outs. That phenomenon didn't begin until after the professional era commenced in 1996. So, if there was an advantage for either team going into the series opener it was with the Lions. This would be the seventh match of their tour.

"I have always said that the best chance to beat the All Blacks is when you are on tour in New Zealand," says Hastings. "That may sound surprising to most people because I'm sure the majority would assume the last place you'd want to do battle with them would be at Eden Park or Carisbrook.

"But the truth is all the matches you play before the first test provide a team with the perfect build-up. Rugby is built into the fabric of New Zealand society. When you're on tour playing teams like Wairarapa Bush and Taranaki you realise that. Playing New Zealand's provincial teams helps prepare you mentally and physically, so going into the first test we were certainly battle-hardened. We'd lost our game against Otago the previous Saturday but I wasn't too worried because it had served as a bit of a wake-up call. We were under no illusions about the battle that awaited us but there was a real belief that we could win."

The test couldn't have got off to a worse start for the Lions. Within the first minute of the game All Black centre Frank Bunce was awarded a controversial try after Kinsey ruled that he had beaten Lions' winger Ieuan Evans to the touchdown. It was to be the only try of a dour match. Hastings and Fox landed six and five penalties apiece and it was the New Zealander's fifth that won the game in dubious circumstances. Kinsey awarded a penalty against Dean Richards for a maul infringement with three minutes left on the clock. Fox's successful kick made the score 20-18 to the All Blacks and left the Lions players and management fuming.

"We were absolutely robbed," says Hastings. "The opening try by Bunce was never a try and the penalty awarded against us at the death was nothing short of a bad joke. If you take away the first three minutes of the test and the last three minutes, we would have won the game convincingly. It's shocking that a test match can be won on the whims of a referee. I'm not making excuses but it was a terrible performance by the referee. There is no way New Zealand should have been given that penalty. I don't care what anyone says, and I certainly don't expect New Zealanders to agree with me, but it was arguably the worst decision made in a match that I played in. I don't think there is any doubt that it cost us the series."

In many ways the resolve the Lions showed in winning the second test 20-7 in Wellington two weeks later was born out of that Lancaster Park frustration. "We knew the All Blacks were lucky to escape with the first-test victory and we all held the genuine belief that we were in no way inferior. When we arrived in Wellington we were determined to prove the point. It would have taken a magnificent effort from the All Blacks to beat us that day. It was one of the best Lions' performances ever on New Zealand soil."

If the second test was a classic Lions' performance, the third test at Eden Park was just as convincing in the All Blacks' favour. Tries by Bunce, Fitzpatrick and halfback Jon Preston helped New Zealand to a 30-13 triumph. The Lions' hopes of matching their 1971 predecessors by winning a test series in New Zealand were gone.

"It was a very disappointing day for us in Auckland," Hastings says. "My heart sinks every time I think about it. I'm not saying the result in Wellington would have been the same if the referee had done his job in Christchurch but it's certainly something I'm sure all of the Lions' players have thought about since. As it was, following our win in Wellington with a test in Auckland seven days later was just too tough. It would have suited us if we'd been given a game against Auckland in between the second and third tests. That would have allowed us an opportunity to come back down from our high. I've always thought it impossible for a team to peak two Saturdays in a row. It's very difficult to maintain the sort of standards you need to beat the All Blacks for consecutive weekends. It is much easier to raise your game from a lower level than it is to maintain the same standards. Certainly we weren't able to come close to the level of our performance at Wellington when we played at Eden Park."

It will come as no surprise that Hastings is an avid advocate for the introduction of video technology to assist referees in making decisions about tries.

"There are too many examples of tries being awarded that simply aren't tries. Obviously, the technology that is available now wasn't around in 1993 but now that it is I absolutely support any moves to introduce it to rugby at the top level. No player should have to walk off the field knowing that he's been cheated out of victory. Frank Bunce's try in Christchurch should never have been given. There is no way on God's earth that he scored that day. A video referee would have proved that and we wouldn't have had victory snatched away from us."

⋅⋅⋅

HASTINGS' last international was against the All Blacks. The venue was Loftus Versfeld in South Africa and the occasion was a World Cup quarter-final. The game was won by the All Blacks 48-30 although, as would be expected from any side with Hastings at the helm, the Scots went down with all guns firing. In the process, they became only the second team in 103 years of All Black rugby to score 30 points against New Zealand. Following the inevitable dressing room TV interview after making his 61st and final appearance for his country, the loyal Scottish fans demanded Hastings re-emerge for an impromptu lap of honour – a jog that ended with him being chaired off to thunderous applause.

There were many tributes on this day. Hastings offered his own for New Zealand's emerging star Jonah Lomu, who turned the quarter-final with a spectacular try. "There's no doubt about it," Hastings told reporters, "he's a big bastard!"

But the most fitting tribute paid in Pretoria that day was from Hastings' friend and rival Fitzpatrick. The All Black captain, choosing his words carefully, paid the ultimate tribute to Hastings when he said *Gavin Hastings' heart and spirit may come from Scotland, but he has the soul of an All Black.*

GAVIN HASTINGS AGAINST THE ALL BLACKS

Date	For	Venue	Result	Score	Points
6-6-87	Scotland	Christchurch	lost	3-30	pen
25-11-89	Barbarians	London	lost	10-21	2 pens
16-6-90	Scotland	Dunedin	lost	16-31	2 cons
23-6-90	Scotland	Auckland	lost	18-21	2 cons, 2 pens
30-10-91	Scotland	Cardiff	lost	6-13	2 pens
18-4-92	World XV	Christchurch	won	28-14	pen
22-4-92	World XV	Wellington	lost	26-54	try
25-4-92	World XV	Auckland	lost	15-26	
12-6-93	British Isles	Christchurch	lost	18-20	6 pens
26-6-93	British Isles	Wellington	won	20-7	4 pens
3-7-93	British Isles	Auckland	lost	13-30	con, 2 pens
20-11-93	Scotland	Edinburgh	lost	15-51	5 pens
11-6-95	Scotland	Pretoria	lost	30-48	3 cons, 3 pens

TEST MATCH CAREER

	P	W	L	D	T	C	P	Dg	Pts
vs All Blacks	9	1	8	-	-	8	25	-	91
All Tests	67	34	31	2	18	87	160	-	733

Phil Kearns

"Hooking against Phil Kearns was a real challenge in the '90s. He's a tough competitor and I enjoyed the rivalry. We brought the best out in each other"

Sean Fitzpatrick
(**Turning Point,** 1998)

Date of birth: 27-6-1967
Born at: Sydney, Australia
Position: Hooker
Test matches: 67

THIS chapter might have been subtitled "The mellowing of rugby's happy hooker". Might have been if Phil Kearns had co-operated and mellowed to any appreciable degree. He hasn't. Oh, he has smoothed out some of the renowned rough edges he displayed in the early '90s when as a young up-and-comer he delivered his now-famous double-fingered salute to New Zealand as he helped that Australian side over-achieve by defeating the All Blacks.

He has tempered the unpredictable, intimidating style he used as he threw himself into rucks before emerging with the ball and galloping up the middle of the park for a well-earned 10-metre spurt. But you wouldn't say the Wallaby great has mellowed.

Any temptation to think so is laid to rest when you hear Kearns muse about the All Blacks. In 1999, after Wallaby coach Rod Macqueen selected his side for the Tri-Nations showdown with the All Blacks at Eden Park, Kearns knew defeat was close. The forward pack Macqueen selected for the test included this front five: props Glenn Panoho and Andrew Blades, hooker Jeremy Paul and locks David Giffin and John Welborn – all were making their first appearances against New Zealand. With Kearns on the reserves bench, the test was lost 35-14. A month later Kearns would return to the line-up and help the Wallabies to a stirring 28-7 win.

"Rod picked what he thought was the best team," says Kearns, "but to go into a test against the All Blacks with a front five short on experience was suicidal. When you play the All Blacks you can't afford to give them an inch. If they smell blood, they'll murder you. The onslaught of an All Black pack that senses a weakness is immense.

"There are things you can do to slow them down but at Eden Park that night Australia had no answers. If you are going to compete against an All Black pack you have to be totally committed. At times you need to have a type of war mentality. You have to fight fire with fire. You get into their faces and compete. You certainly don't take a step backwards.

"I know the players selected for that test tried as hard as they could but by the time we got back into it in the second half, the game was over. It was a mighty effort by the All Blacks. I can't say I was surprised... I'd seen it all before."

ﻩﻩ

HE has never feared the All Blacks. Respected them for sure, but never feared them. Which is surprising when you remember his first match for Australia was against an All Black team that was undefeated for 16 internationals when Kearns ran out onto Eden Park in a one-off Bledisloe Cup test in 1989. The match was a remarkable one for Kearns for a number of reasons. Coach Bob Dwyer – his position under threat after a 2-1 series loss to the British Lions – plucked Kearns from the Randwick reserve grade team for the test. Along with prop Tony Daly and second-five Tim Horan, Kearns was one of three new caps selected as Dwyer attempted to get the planning for the 1991 World Cup right. Kearns was brought into the fold at the expense of his idol Tommy Lawton. Another player called back into the Wallaby side was 50-test veteran flanker Simon Poidevin. Dwyer roomed the old hand with the new hooker in the build-up to the test.

"Everyone talked about the aura of the All Black team," says Kearns, "but at that time it didn't exist for me. I could sense that the older players, like Simon, had a tremendous respect for the All Blacks and everything they represented but, to be honest, it was a little beyond me. The respect for the traditions of the All Blacks and the regard for the way they play the game came later in my career.

"When I joined the squad for that first test I didn't really know too much about the All Blacks. I knew they were a great side but that was it. There was no fear or anything like that. I'd been picked out of reserve grade to play in the test so making my debut was daunting – but it would have been daunting whoever the opposition was. It didn't really matter to me, or impress me, that my first game was going to be against New Zealand."

Kearns' disregard for the All Black jersey at the time wasn't born out of an Australian arrogance that so many New Zealanders like to place on their trans-Tasman rivals. It's just that Kearns hadn't grown up as a rugby fan. He played in the junior ranks at Randwick but his heroes were league players like Ray Price and Steve Rogers. Indeed, Kearns didn't even know that the great Kangaroo forward Price had played eight tests for the Wallabies before switching codes and ending up in his footy card collection.

"I guess I was a rugby player dreaming league dreams," he says. "Rugby certainly didn't have the profile in Australia then that it has now. On Monday mornings at school we'd all be talking about the Winfield Cup. We certainly weren't talking about what the Wallabies were doing."

Kearns' appreciation of everything All Black began to take shape almost immediately his debut test began. Flanked by Daly and Andy McIntyre (playing his 31st and last test), Kearns joined a front row conflict against the battle-hardened Richard Loe, Sean Fitzpatrick and Steve McDowell. Fitzpatrick welcomed the debutants with some classic trash talk: *What are you boys doing here? Go back home to your mothers, fatties.*

Both Kearns and Daly responded with performances that gave

an early insight into a potential that within two seasons (with the eventual addition of Ewen McKenzie) would see them take over from that day's opponents as the world's best front row. But despite the newcomers claiming parity in the battle up front, the All Blacks continued their unbeaten run with a 24-12 victory – New Zealand's fifth consecutive win against Australia.

"Confidence in the Australian side was reasonably high before the test despite the fact that we'd been beaten in a series by the Lions," says Kearns. "There was a real belief among the guys that we could win. We certainly didn't go into the match thinking that we were going to lose. But the All Blacks showed that day that they were a level ahead of us. They knew how to punish any mistakes from their opponents.

"I didn't walk off the field in awe of the All Blacks but I certainly had a whole lot of respect for test rugby. I knew that some of my teammates that day – guys like Poidevin, Nick Farr-Jones, Steve Cutler, Bill Campbell, Steve Tuynman, Michael Lynagh and David Campese – had played in a series-winning team against the All Blacks in 1986 and I remember convincing myself that I would go away and work harder than I ever had because I was determined to aspire to those levels as well."

Kearns' chance to join the elite list of Wallabies who have won a series against their arch-rivals came the following season when an under-pressure Australian team fronted up for a three-test series in New Zealand. Despite arriving in New Zealand after dispatching the touring French side 2-1, the manner of the 28-19 third test loss meant that Dwyer's position at the helm of Wallaby rugby was under threat.

And it wasn't long into the tour before Dwyer came under more fire from the touring Australian media – the Wallabies opened the tour with consecutive losses to Waikato and Auckland before losing the first test 21-6 in Christchurch. It had been a terrible Wallaby performance. Fitzpatrick, Kieran Crowley, Craig Innes and John Kirwan all scored tries as the Australians were outclassed.

"It was one of the worst Wallaby performances I've been involved in," says Kearns. "To this day I can't put my finger on why we played so badly. We didn't approach the game the way we should have. We were a bit blasé about it. It was almost as though we were waiting for them to go off the boil before having a crack at them. My appreciation for All Black rugby was certainly growing."

Dwyer, incensed by the ineptitude of his side in Christchurch, axed five players and made two positional changes for the second test in Auckland. To gauge how annoyed Dwyer was by the first test disaster, it's interesting to note that the five players dropped – fullback Greg Martin, winger Ian Williams, centre Paul Cornish, flanker Steve Tuynman and lock Peter FitzSimons – would never pull on the gold jersey again.

While the changes didn't halt the unbeaten streak of the All Blacks, now at 23 tests, the Australians' 27-17 loss was an improvement from the woeful first test. Without doubt the Wallabies were showing signs of recovery. The forward effort had improved, thanks largely to the performance from first-time tourist Willie Ofahengaue, and as a result the Wallaby backs had more opportunities to unleash the back three of Paul Carozza, John Flett and Campese.

"By the time the third test came around we knew we could compete," says Kearns. "We'd shown enough signs in Auckland that if things went our way we had nothing to fear. There was a real feeling of belief within the team. We honestly thought we could win. Up until then, the series had been a complete disaster. The All Blacks had already clinched the series but for some reason we still believed in each other."

Maybe they believed in each other because they knew that unless they beat the All Blacks in the third test at Wellington they'd be heading into a World Cup year with a new coach. Queensland's John Connolly was already being talked about as a potential replacement. There is no question that it was a desperate Wallaby team that took the field at Athletic Park.

History records that the determined Wallabies won the test 21-9, ending a 50-game All Black unbeaten streak stretching back to the second test against France in 1986. It was that day that Dwyer's young guns came of age. It was also the day that Kearns imprinted himself in the memories of every New Zealander watching – either at the ground or on television. The second half had been in progress for only two minutes when Australia grabbed a 10-9 lead. At a lineout two metres from the New Zealand line, Fitzpatrick threw to his captain Gary Whetton, who lost control of the ball and Kearns swooped on it to score the game's only try. Kearns then leaped to his feet and, while giving his two-fingered salute to Fitzpatrick and All Black halfback Graeme Bachop, bellowed at the top of his voice *Have a nice fucking day, boys!*

"Do I regret it? Of course I do. I usually don't carry on like that after I score a try but for some reason that day I felt like saying something. It is quite embarrassing looking back at videotapes from that day. I am always being reminded about it. I think most Australians have forgotten about it but every time I'm in New Zealand there are usually a few characters who like to remind me what I did."

What Kearns did that day – other than earn the wrath of the New Zealand public – was offer the Wallabies a World Cup lifeline. Dwyer was assured of keeping his job and the team had been given a mighty boost in confidence.

"There's no question the third-test victory was a turning point for us," Kearns says. "We'd finally proved to ourselves that the All Blacks were beatable. That was a massive weight off our shoulders."

Kearns returned to Australia without fulfilling his dream of gaining that elusive series victory, but in 14 months' time he would be a part of something much more special.

※

GARY WHETTON'S short reign as All Black captain was not particularly memorable. It could be argued that few other captains of the modern era had such a negative impact on the position. According to some players of the time, if you weren't a part of his all-conquering Auckland team, you were often ignored. Certainly his All Black teams were defined by cliques. There were the long-time Auckland All Blacks like Steve McDowell, Sean Fitzpatrick, Michael Jones, Zinzan Brooke, Alan Whetton, Grant Fox and John Kirwan, who were treated as equals. There were Auckland teammates like Terry Wright and Craig Innes and senior All Blacks like Richard Loe and Graeme Bachop, who were tolerated. And then there were the rest. It was not a happy All Black team that headed to England for the 1991 World Cup. An arrogance oozed from the Auckland connection within the camp. It was an arrogance that would prove to be the team's downfall. It was an arrogance that their rivals thrived on.

"People like to say that All Black team were an unhappy one," says Kearns. "Obviously, the decision to put Alex Wyllie and John Hart in dual coaching roles added fuel to that fire. But unhappy isn't the word I'd use to describe the 1991 All Blacks. We all thought they were conceited; they were up themselves.

"There is a very fine line between being confident and being arrogant but there is no question that you can be confident without being arrogant. The line is very thin. I'm not sure where the definition starts and where it finishes but I guess the easiest way to draw that line is how you treat other people and what respect you show others.

"When we were in Dublin preparing for the semifinal it was obvious the Irish were on our side – even though we'd beaten Ireland in the quarter-final. I don't think it's an over-reaction to say that they hated the All Blacks. They hated the way that they refused to mix with the locals. They would shut themselves off from the public. It was as though the All Blacks thought they were bigger than the game. As far as I'm concerned some of them absolutely thought they were bigger than the game. Our respect for them as a team hadn't diminished but our respect for them as individuals had."

By the time the World Cup semifinal came around, the aura that the All Blacks had enjoyed within the mind game between the two teams had diminished as well. There had been two tests since the end of the 1990 series in New Zealand – Australia winning 21-12 in Sydney and the All Blacks winning a dour kicking duel between Grant Fox and Michael Lynagh 6-3 in Auckland. Unquestionably, the Eden Park test had been winnable for the Australians but an off day from the normally reliable Lynagh, who offered up a career low percentage of one success from seven attempts at goal, sunk their chances.

There was a feeling within the Australian team that All Black confidence was misplaced. When the sides had played in Sydney two months earlier, the weaknesses in the All Black team were exposed. The days of parity between the front rows were over. Kearns, Ewen McKenzie and Tony Daly dominated their opposites while the Wallabies' back rowers Simon Poidevin, Willie Ofahengaue and Tim Gavin were more effective than their All Black counterparts Michael Jones, Zinzan Brooke and Andy Earl. And in the backs, Australia's dynamic duo of Nick Farr-Jones and Lynagh finally had some hardened support outside them. Tim Horan and

Jason Little provided stellar midfield defence as well as an appreciation for flair on attack – something New Zealand's midfield of Bernie McCahill and Craig Innes were lacking.

"That aura was gone," says Kearns. "There was still a healthy respect but going into the World Cup we'd won two of the last three tests against them. It didn't matter to us that we'd struggled to beat the Irish. We hadn't played our best rugby in the quarter-final but going into the semi that didn't matter. It was us against the All Blacks and there was no chance that any of us would feel intimidated by the opposition. We sensed they were confident, sensed they were arrogantly over-confident, which was surprising because they didn't have anything from the tests earlier that year to suggest that they would dominate the semifinal."

By the 35th minute of the semifinal the Wallabies held a 13-0 lead after a majestic display from Campese saw him score a 12th-minute try then set up Horan for a second. The final score would be 16-6 and Australia, a week later, would beat England 12-6 in the final.

"When you lose that aura that everyone associates with your team, it is very hard to get it back," says Kearns. "In many ways, we destroyed all the myths about the great All Black team when we beat them in Wellington in 1990. That victory, and the one in Sydney in 1991, ensured that every Australian in that semifinal had tasted victory against the All Blacks.

"We knew we had nothing to fear. Even some of the older guys who'd been a part of the series win in 1986 needed to be a part of the more recent victories to re-establish their belief in themselves and the team. As far as that era of Wallaby rugby was concerned, we were now the team to be feared."

And so it proved. By the time the teams met again the following year in a three-test series in Australia, Kearns was all but guaranteed that elusive series win. The All Blacks, with Laurie Mains at the helm and Fitzpatrick installed as captain, were very much in a rebuilding phase. But despite seven All Blacks playing against the Wallabies for the first time, Mains' team put up a brave fight in the series.

The first test in Sydney was won 16-15 when a 71st-minute Lynagh penalty gave Australia the win and the series was clinched two weeks later in Brisbane when Paul Carozza scored a 70th-minute try to give the Wallabies a 19-17 victory.

"We were the world champions and now we had the Bledisloe Cup," says Kearns. "It was a fantastic feeling. But it also served as a bit of a wake-up call. There were a lot of new faces in the All Blacks that year but they were just as competitive as they had been a year earlier. I'd heard people say that there is no such thing as a bad All Black side and now I knew what they'd meant. Some All Black teams play better than others, but you underestimate an All Black side at your peril."

Much of the credit for the All Blacks' strong showing in the series – Mains' team won the third test in Sydney 26-23 – was due to Fitzpatrick's captaincy. He was still learning his trade but his combative attitude meant that he was a natural leader of men. His players wanted to follow him. It was a quality Kearns shared when he took on the Australian captaincy four months after the series during the side's northern hemisphere tour. Both men were the equal of each other when it came to heart, edge and defiance.

"I have an enormous respect for Sean Fitzpatrick," says Kearns. "The thing I admire the most about him is his competitive nature. It didn't matter if I played against him when he was wearing the Auckland jersey or the All Black jersey – every game against him was as tough as the last one. He never let his performance waver. I always knew a game against a team that Fitzy was in was going to be bloody hard.

"He would have made a great referee as well. He never stopped talking. He seemed to know every rule in the book... and if he didn't he'd just make one up and hope the ref would go along with him!

"Early on in my career he talked a bit of trash talk but as we played more and more against each other he toned down the rubbish. We'd still have a go at each other – if the All Black scrum was dominating us he'd say something sarcastic like *Good scrum Kearnsy!* But it was all light-hearted stuff.

"There's no question that if I was selecting a team to play as a World XV he would be one of the first names on the list. The guy should be revered in New Zealand. He's a treasure."

Fitzpatrick won the first battle between them as captains in 1993 when the All Blacks won 25-10 in Dunedin. Kearns evened the score the following season when, thanks to a 76th-minute desperation tackle from halfback George Gregan on Jeff Wilson, Australia landed a thrilling 20-16 Bledisloe Cup triumph.

While the Australian captaincy was offered to the returning Michael Lynagh for the 1995 World Cup – Australia was beaten in a quarter-final by England while New Zealand lost to South Africa in the final – Kearns regained the position for the two post-World Cup tests between the Australasian powers. Both tests were won by New Zealand – the Auckland game 28-16 and the return match in Sydney 34-23. It would be the last time these two great hooking rivals played against each other in the test arena. Fitzpatrick's career would end late in 1997 when a knee injury brought down the curtain on a career that spanned 91 tests while Kearns would be knocked out of international rugby for two years with an Achilles tendon injury and then a crippling knee complaint.

❧

SUDDENLY everything that had come before acquired a purpose. The struggle with injury: not that bad. The self-doubt: laced with dreams of success. The failed comebacks: a comeback worth dreaming about.

When Phil Kearns rejoined the Wallaby side in 1998 he couldn't have dreamed what was about to unfold. In the time that he was out of international rugby the Wallabies had hired and fired coach Greg Smith and lost an incredible five consecutive tests to the All Blacks. When the team assembled in Melbourne for the first Tri-Nations test of the year, the only survivors of Australia's last win against New Zealand, in 1994, were George Gregan, David Wilson, John Eales and Kearns.

But if Kearns was expecting to assist his captain Eales in trying to convince his new teammates that it was possible to beat the All Blacks, he need not have worried.

"I was expecting to give the same advice to the younger players that I was given when I played against the All Blacks for the first time. I can remember Simon Poidevin telling me to forget about all the things I may have heard about the All Blacks. He talked about the game being between two teams of 15 players. He wanted to play down the myth of the All Blacks, play down the black jersey, play down all the traditions that go along with New Zealand rugby.

"But there was no need for me to pass on any advice. I don't know if it's because of the professional era but the new breed of Wallaby have a real self-confidence. They don't seem to need the reassurance that I needed when I was younger. It didn't matter to them that we hadn't beaten the All Blacks for three seasons. They were only interested in what could happen now. There was an abundance of controlled confidence in the squad when the All Blacks rolled into town."

There were plenty of reasons for confidence. Australia's new coach Rod Macqueen is one of the game's great man-managers and he wasn't afraid to make changes from Smith's last squad. Regular fullback Stephen Larkham was asked to play at first-five, while centre Daniel Herbert, No 8 Toutai Kefu, flanker Matt Cockbain, lock Tom Bowman and Kearns were added to the starting line-up. Another reason for the Australian confidence was that the All Blacks were venturing into an international season without Sean Fitzpatrick for the first time since 1987. The great No 8 Zinzan Brooke and inspirational centre Frank Bunce were also missing. All had retired and, with the exception of new hooker Anton Oliver, none of the replacements at that time was worthy of lacing their predecessors' boots.

As it was, the whipping boys of the Bledisloe Cup – Australia had lost the last seven tests between the two countries – recorded a 24-16 win at the Melbourne Cricket Ground. Three weeks later, in Christchurch, Macqueen's men won 27-23, securing the country's first win on New Zealand soil since 1990 as well as the Bledisloe. And before New Zealanders had the chance to catch their breath, the Wallabies swept the All Blacks with a come-from-behind 19-14 win at the Sydney Football Stadium – joining Tommy Lawton's 1929 Australian side as the only team to defeat the All Blacks 3-0.

"It made all the difficulties of getting through the injuries worth while," says Kearns. "There were times when I had to stop myself from thinking that I would never play again. But to be able to come back and be a part of an Australian side to beat the All Blacks 3-0 was beyond my wildest dreams.

"It meant so much to me because I have been involved in so many battles against the All Blacks down the years which have been lost. You learn very quickly to cherish every win because a win against the Blacks can be very rare. It's a tribute to New Zealand rugby that despite the tests we play against the British Lions and the South Africans, it is the games against the All Blacks that matter most. New Zealanders probably regard the South Africans as their greatest rivals but for Australians the All Blacks pose the greatest challenge.

"The black jersey is something to be respected. But it's nice to know that, for a seven-week stretch in 1998, it was the green and gold jersey that earned the respect of the All Blacks."

PHIL KEARNS AGAINST THE ALL BLACKS

Date	For	Venue	Result	Score	Points
5-8-89	Australia	Auckland	lost	12-24	
21-7-90	Australia	Christchurch	lost	6-21	
4-8-90	Australia	Auckland	lost	17-27	
18-8-90	Australia	Wellington	won	21-9	try
10-8-91	Australia	Sydney	won	21-12	
24-8-91	Australia	Auckland	lost	3-6	
27-10-91	Australia	Dublin	won	16-6	
18-4-92	World XV	Christchurch	won	24-18	
22-4-92	World XV	Wellington	lost	26-54	
25-4-92	World XV	Auckland	lost	15-26	
4-7-92	Australia	Sydney	won	16-15	
19-7-92	Australia	Brisbane	won	19-17	
25-7-92	Australia	Sydney	lost	23-26	
17-7-93	Australia	Dunedin	lost	10-25	
17-8-94	Australia	Sydney	won	20-16	
22-7-95	Australia	Auckland	lost	16-28	
29-7-95	Australia	Sydney	lost	23-34	
11-7-98	Australia	Melbourne	won	24-16	
1-8-98	Australia	Christchurch	won	27-23	
29-8-98	Australia	Sydney	won	19-14	
28-8-99	Australia	Sydney	won	28-7	

TEST MATCH CAREER

	W	L	D	T	C	P	Dg	Pts
vs All Blacks	18	10	8	-	1	-	-	-	4
All Tests	65	48	17	-	8	-	-	-	34

Willie John McBride

"Willie John McBride was a great competitor... few scrums would have had a more devoted, fired-up core man"

Colin Meads
(**Colin Meads All Black,** 1974)

Date of birth: 6-6-1940
Born at: Toomebridge, Ireland
Position: Lock
Test matches: 80

WHEN he threw the punch he didn't know too much about the All Black standing next to him in the lineout. It didn't matter to him that the punching bag just happened to be the most famous All Black of all. When the punch connected, you could hear the sighs from the Lansdowne Road crowd. They knew the revenge swing wouldn't be too far away.

"I didn't know who the hell Colin Meads was," says Willie John McBride. "The only thing I knew was that he was a big bugger who never stopped chipping away at the referee. During the lineouts he kept infringing so I decided to give him one. A few minutes later, when I was in a ruck, I was smashed in the face. I knew who threw it, too. I never saw him throw it, but it was Meads all right. Only

Meads could have thrown a punch like that... he would have been a good boxer."

The incident during the 1963 All Black test against Ireland in Dublin was the beginning of a rivalry that would last nine more seasons. But it was a rivalry based on respect rather than confrontation.

"It wasn't a gentlemen's agreement but we never really had a crack at each other after that," says McBride. "We didn't get together and make a decision not to hit each other again... it was just born out of the respect we held for each other. You know what players are worth. You know what they will take and how you will take it. I knew, after one game against him, that Meads was something special. There was an aura about him. There were a lot of great All Black players in those days but they were all in Meads' shadow. When I walked off the park that day I had a great admiration for him. I knew that I'd just played against a legend."

McBride would have been one of the few, if not the only, person at Lansdowne Rd that day who didn't know of the legend that was Colin Meads. To understand McBride you must first realise that he was not brought up with rugby in his blood. While Welsh great Cliff Morgan admits the two things he learned on his grandmother's knee were the Lord's Prayer and that All Black Bob Deans did in fact score in 1905, McBride's family had no tradition or background in sport.

McBride did not start playing rugby until his final year of high school. His father had died when he was four and there was little time for anything other than working on the farm along with his mother, three brothers and sister. And it's that background on the farm that helped him forge a close relationship with Meads.

"I identified with him because we came from similar backgrounds," says McBride. "Neither of us grew up with a lot of niceties. We had to work on the farm while our friends were out doing other things. We both came to rugby understanding what hard work was.

"It's not an easy thing being an All Black. It's a lot of years of hard work. You have to deny yourself a lot of things to get to the top. You can't go and get drunk with your friends, you have to

Unbridled joy for France's Serge Blanco after his match-winning try against Australia in the 1987 World Cup semifinal in Sydney.

Andrew Cornaga, Photosport

David Campese offers his Wallaby teammates advice during his last test outing in New Zealand at Athletic Park in 1996. All Campese's words, however, counted for nought as the Aussies suffered a record 43-6 defeat in the Bledisloe Cup-Tri Nations match.

David Campese keeps a wary eye on proceedings during the 1993 Bledisloe Cup clash at Carisbrook. The All Blacks won this match 25-10.

Scottish superboot Gavin Hastings lines up a kick at goal during the 1995 World Cup. Hastings scored 227 points for Scotland over three World Cup tournaments.

Another day at the office... battle weary Phil Kearns retires to the dressing-room after Australia's 21-12 win in the opening Bledisloe Cup match of 1991 in Sydney. The All Blacks came back to win the second test at Eden Park, but the Wallabies had the last laugh of 1991 in the World Cup semifinal at Lansdowne Road, Dublin.

No Moore, please! England hooker Brian Moore shows signs of strain during
the World Cup semifinal against the All Blacks at Cape Town, 1995.

François Pienaar raises the Webb Ellis Trophy after the Springboks' epic 15-12 win over the All Blacks in the 1995 World Cup final in Johannesburg.

Gary Teichmann sprints free of the All Black defence during the 1997 Tri Nations series.

get used to being away from your family... there are a lot of sacrifices that must be made. And because he was from the King Country he didn't have the advantage of the things the big city offered. He was successful, but nothing was ever handed to him. I saw a lot of myself in him."

It's a tribute to McBride that the similarities between the two men did not end off the field. Both men were combative, front-of-the-lineout jumpers. Both enjoyed the hard, physical confrontations that rugby offered and while the fists didn't fly between the two following the first flourish, theirs was a rivalry that captured the imagination of two countries every time they faced up to each other.

"He was a shrewd man," says McBride. "He was a thorn in the flesh of every team he played against because he had a knack of upsetting the opposition. And he was tough – as tough as they come. It didn't matter how hard you knocked him down or how hard you hit him, he was back up off the ground and in your face straight away. He was one of those players who never laid down."

McBride's introduction to Meads and All Black rugby was a baptism of fire. Despite the All Blacks needing a second-half penalty from Don Clarke to escape with a 6-5 win, the New Zealand forwards dominated the game, creating plenty of attacking opportunities for a backline that included two debutants – Auckland winger Malcolm Dick and Canterbury centre Derek Arnold.

Says McBride: "By the time I left the field I knew, in no uncertain terms, what the All Blacks were about. Before the game I knew they were a good team but that's all I knew. I was a bit naive when it came to the All Blacks. Some of my teammates had talked about the great players who had worn the black jersey in the past but that meant nothing to me.

"But by the end of the day I had masses of respect for them. The intensity they played with was like nothing I'd seen before. The All Blacks didn't take a backward step all day. It was inspiring to see what pulling on that black jersey meant to every one of them. It's a good thing we played with a lot of passion because, if we hadn't, it would have been a romp."

THE irony is this... Willie John McBride had the misfortune to hit rock bottom in two whitewashed Lions series against the All Blacks – in 1966 as a player and again in 1983 as a manager. Neither team managed a test win in the four-test series. Both sides returned home as laughing stocks of both the New Zealand and British press. But through it all, McBride emerged unscathed. His pride was hurt, yes. He was frustrated, yes. His reputation was shot, never.

"There is something you learn very quickly when you play with Willie John," says Gareth Edwards, his Lions teammate in 1971. "He is a leader of men. If things go wrong on the field you can always be sure that Willie John isn't a part of the problem. He's the one trying to put things right. Every team have their leaders, but there will only ever be one Willie John."

The 1966 tour by the Lions was without doubt the low point of McBride's career. Despite the side winning their two tests in Australia on the way to New Zealand – they beat the Wallabies 11-8 in Sydney before cruising to a 31-0 win in Brisbane – the Lions proved no match for an All Black team which had been so impressive in the previous year when they'd won a hard-fought series against the powerful Springboks.

McBride's chances of selection weren't helped by the peculiar decision to make Scotland lock Mike Campbell-Lamerton captain. With Welshman Brian Price filling the other locking spot, McBride missed the tests in Australia and was instructed to play either on the blindside or at No 8 in the midweek games.

"Right from the start of the New Zealand section of the tour, I knew we were in trouble," says McBride. "We'd been led into a false sense of security in Australia. The sun was shining, we were playing on hard grounds with a dry ball and we were winning games. To then be in Invercargill in the wet and cold with the opposition at fever pitch, we were suddenly in a lot of trouble."

By the time the first test in Dunedin rolled round, the Lions had suffered losses to Southland, Otago and Wellington and had been lucky in escaping against Bay of Plenty with a scrappy draw.

The test was a one-sided affair. The All Blacks, with tries from Bruce McLeod, Mick Williment and Brian Lochore, cruised to a 20-3 win, with the only Lions' points coming from a Stewart Wilson penalty.

But if the Lions' performance on the field was a bumbling one, the Lions' management actually managed a worse job off the field. In an effort to combat the All Black pack, Lions coach John Robins added McBride to the side to partner Wales' Delme Thomas in the locking positions. The new pairing was a great success as the Lions held the All Blacks to 16-12 in the second test at Athletic Park.

"We had a chance to win that game," says McBride. "The All Blacks at that time were a well-oiled machine. It didn't matter where you looked to attack them, they always seemed to have such fantastic depth. But despite that, we'd been competitive. I wouldn't say we matched them in the forwards but we got as close as that group of players could have got. We were down 0-2 but after that performance we felt like we had a chance of at least sneaking one of the two remaining tests."

Any chance of continuity within the Lions' camp was shattered when Robins announced the team for the third test at Lancaster Park. Campbell-Lamerton, hopelessly outplayed by Colin Meads in the first test, was reinstated with Thomas moved to the front row. In contrast, the All Blacks fielded an unchanged line-up for the third consecutive test.

"The tour was just one mistake after another," says McBride. "Moving Delme Thomas to the front row was just another example of how amateurish we were in our approach. There wasn't a lot of thought going into management or organisation of the tour. As a result we got smashed. It was very difficult to take. I'm not saying we would have been good enough to beat the All Blacks had the selections been better, but we may have been able to walk off the track with our heads held higher than they were."

Two tries by Waka Nathan and one from Tony Steel helped secure a 19-6 win before the fourth test – when Campbell-Lamerton was again replaced (this time by Brian Price) – once more saw a convincingly win, 24-11, to New Zealand.

"I remember coming home from the tour and making a promise to myself that if I ever went back to New Zealand, I would never let myself be a part of such a divided and unprofessional team. We had some good players on the tour, but it didn't help that, as soon as things started to go wrong, the different groups of guys from Wales, Ireland, Scotland and England started to blame each other. We were completely and utterly out of our depth, both on the field and off. It was a sad time to be a Lion."

The saving grace for McBride is the knowledge that the Lions had come up against arguably one of the best All Black sides to take the field.

Colin Meads was at the peak of his career, as was his locking partner and brother Stan. And with names like Waka Nathan, Kel Tremain, Brian Lochore, Chris Laidlaw and Ian MacRae in the side, there was no shortage of power and talent. McBride, in his debut against the All Blacks in 1963, had also lined up against the legendary All Black captain Wilson Whineray. The opportunity to play against men of that calibre is something still treasured.

"If I could relive my rugby career and was able to choose the era that I played in, I wouldn't change a thing," he says. "Men like Whineray, Lochore, Tremain… they were all in the Colin Meads mould. They were so talented but they never forgot they were members of a team. They weren't show-offs. Whineray was a great man who got tremendous respect from the players around him. Lochore was similar to Colin Meads. He was a big, strong man who just never lay down.

"The remarkable thing about the All Blacks at the time was that they got into trouble in the odd game. With five minutes to go, you'd put your house on them losing but it was through sheer doggedness and a refuse-to-lose attitude, that they would score a try, drop a goal or get a penalty to win the game. And invariably it would be people like Lochore or Tremain or later on a fellow like Ian Kirkpatrick who would suddenly appear in the last few minutes of a match with energy that no one else on the field had left. They were those types of players; so fit and so skilled.

"It is difficult to watch the All Blacks these days and compare them with guys I played against. Okay, today's players may be more skilful but the guys I played against *were* men. In the era I played in we weren't allowed to get hurt. There were no substitutions, you just had to stay on the field unless you broke your neck. When you got hurt you didn't let people see that you were hurt. Today you don't even need to play 80 minutes. If a guy has a headache, he's told not to play!

"But the All Blacks, the real All Blacks, they didn't know what pain was. Colin Meads played different games with a broken arm and a broken hand. We all suffered pain but we'd work through those barriers. I remember playing against him when he was playing for King Country. I knew he had bruised ribs and when he came to the first lineout I looked at him and he had a scowl on his face. I told him *Don't come any closer or you'll get another one on your ribs!* He just looked at me, grunted, winked and carried on.

"It was no wonder that every boy's dream in New Zealand was to be an All Black. They had so many heroes to choose from. That's something Ireland has never had. There's never been a rugby fever here. There's passion, and on our day that can help Ireland beat the better teams, but there's no rugby fever here."

SOMETIMES even the great players have to lie to themselves. The occasions are rare but nonetheless the lie still has to be believed.

That was certainly the case when in 1983 McBride took charge of the management of the touring Lions' team. The side were humiliated with four consecutive test losses – 16-12 in Christchurch, 9-0 in Wellington, 15-8 in Christchurch and 38-6 in Auckland.

"We were never going to win the series but you can't give in to reality," says McBride. "If I'd given in to reality I probably would never have even made the trip! We were that bad. The 1983 Five Nations championship was total rubbish. We actually struggled to find 30 players up to the task of touring New Zealand."

It was like turning the clock back to 1966 for McBride. And five years after that tour, the self-doubt remained on the eve of the 1971 Lions' tour.

"When the Lions were named I had a difficult time believing we could win," says McBride. "I was probably still suffering a little from the drubbing we'd got five years earlier. The All Blacks had been so powerful then and I knew there was a massive challenge ahead of us."

McBride's doubt was well-founded. Since the 4-0 slaying of the Lions in 1966, the All Blacks had played Wales three times and had one-off tests against England and Scotland, recording five victories. It was, in fact, the Welsh players who helped convince McBride that a series win in New Zealand was possible.

"The Welsh were years ahead of Ireland, Scotland and England," says McBride. "The organisation of the coaching set-up in Wales was second-to-none and as a result they had a host of world-class players just itching to have another crack at the All Blacks. It was very difficult not to be confident when you were surrounded by guys like Gareth Edwards, Barry John and JPR Williams. These guys were in a class of their own. The New Zealand media tried to brand them as being arrogant but, let's be honest, playing good rugby is all a matter of confidence. If you believe you can win, you are halfway there.

"Because the Welsh contingent in the side was so dominant, it made it very easy for the other guys within the squad to feel a part of things because there was a lot of admiration for Welsh rugby at the time. If the Welsh players had been ignored by the selectors and English players had dominated the squad, well, there would have been problems. But as it was there was a team spirit in that Lions' team that I hadn't experienced before."

As in 1966, the pressure of a Lions' tour got to the selectors but this time it was the New Zealanders who panicked. It was obvious even before a ball had been kicked that the Lions had the upper hand in the backs. With the international retirement of All Black centres Ian MacRae and Grahame Thorne after the series in South Africa in 1970, the heart of the New Zealand backline was decimated. As a result, Bryan Williams was asked to play in the centres to help combat the Lions' centre pairing of John Dawes and Mike Gibson. Williams had played in the centres in the third test against the Springboks but it was widely regarded as a failure. As far as the Lions were concerned the All Blacks had taken their most lethal winger and nullified him.

"We weren't complaining," says McBride. "Williams was a fantastic player and it seemed like a strange move at the time. I know that John Dawes and Mike Gibson were happy about it. But I knew that the dominance of the backs wasn't going to win us the series on its own. The forward pack had to stand up and be counted."

It did. So much so that with the series tied 1-1 after the All Blacks had answered a 3-9 loss in Dunedin with a 22-12 win in Christchurch, the All Black selectors brought Brian Lochore out of retirement to play as locking partner to Colin Meads in Wellington. The move was a disaster. Lochore, who should be credited for answering his country's call in its time of need, added nothing to the All Black scrum and despite some first-rate work in the loose from Ian Kirkpatrick and Alex Wyllie, the New Zealand forwards were a poor second to the Lions' pack as the visitors won 13-3.

With Peter Whiting restored at lock in place of Lochore for the fourth test at Eden Park, hopes were high the All Blacks could level the series. Despite the dominance of their backs, there were still question marks over the Lions pack. Their defence had been stellar in Wellington, but there was a feeling that it was only a matter of time before the Lions' resolve would crack under the expected onslaught from Kirkpatrick, Wyllie and the recalled Tom Lister.

"To be honest, we didn't play that well," says McBride. "We didn't play as well as we thought we were going to and we certainly didn't do the things that we had planned to do. We were struggling and at one stage it looked like the All Blacks would be good enough to level the series."

While there is little doubt the hero of the day was fullback JPR Williams who nailed a 40-metre drop goal to help secure a 14-14 draw and the Lions' first series win in New Zealand, McBride doesn't under-estimate the role played by rugged All Black prop 'Jaz' Muller.

"He kept us in the game. I'd like to think we put him under a lot of pressure but Muller did a lot of stupid things that day. He kept kicking guys on the ground and giving us penalties. We weren't that much better than the All Blacks that day but his stupidity certainly helped our cause."

Muller would never play for the All Blacks again, and the Auckland test also marked the end of the road for Colin Meads, who had captained the All Blacks in the series. And in the middle of the euphoria of the Lions' series win, McBride found time to console his great rival.

"There is no question that being a part of the Lions' side that day provided me with one of the great highlights of my career," he says. "But at the same time, there was sadness for Meads. He had been such a warrior for the All Blacks. He deserved a better send-off to his career. His career was one that should have ended on a high. Even though he wouldn't have liked it, Meads' career deserved to end with him being hoisted up by his teammates after a series win.

"Despite the sad end, he was a champion that day. He accepted defeat and came into our dressing room, shook everyone's hand and drank a toast to the Lions. I've known a few captains who would not have been so gracious."

The next time McBride played the All Blacks came two years later in Dublin. The New Zealanders, after recording wins against Wales, Scotland and England, were beginning to feel the effects of a tour that had started more than two months earlier. Since their 9-0 win at Twickenham the All Blacks had struggled to a 20-15 win against Newport, defeated a Midland Counties side 43-12 and stumbled to a 3-3 draw with Munster.

Ireland went into the test with an experienced line-up. Captain and fullback Tom Kiernan had been on hand with McBride and prop Ray McLoughlin when the Irish last hosted New Zealand 10 years earlier, while hooker Ken Kennedy, prop Sean Lynch, flanker Fergus Slattery and midfield back Mike Gibson had all been to New Zealand on Lions duty.

That experience and a dose of famous Irish passion saw the home side earn a famous 10-10 draw.

"It wasn't a victory but it was a moral victory," says McBride. "There's no way in hell that Ireland should ever beat the All Blacks. Sure, we had some very good players in those days, but that All Black team with men like Ian Kirkpatrick, Alex Wyllie, Sid Going, Bryan Williams: these guys were fantastic players. It was a little strange playing against an All Black team without Colin Meads but it didn't seem to bother the New Zealanders. At times it seems as though there must be a conveyor belt somewhere in New Zealand with great All Blacks just rolling off.

"That's one of the things I find fascinating about All Black rugby.

Others will talk about the black jersey and the haka. Well, the colour of the jersey certainly never bothered me and I never knew what the haka meant. I didn't mind it... if the All Blacks wanted to sing a little song before playing a test that was up to them. The thing that impressed me more than anything about New Zealand rugby is that there has never been a bad All Black side.

"Every other country goes through massive swings of highs and lows. Of course, some All Black sides are better than others, but the standard is always high. Even in 1998 when the All Blacks lost five tests in a row I don't think you could call the side a bad one. The players were very good players. Maybe the coach was a little more responsible for the poor form.

"But regardless, the high standard of the All Blacks means that through history they have been extremely consistent. It's something that Ireland has never been able to achieve. If you have a bad game in the green jersey the chances are you'll be back the next weekend. If you have a bad game in the All Black jersey, you're out! That kind of pressure on the players is healthy. It's the pressure that leads to consistency."

The lack of consistency in Irish rugby was exposed in 1974 when the All Blacks headed to Lansdowne Road to take part in Ireland's centenary celebrations. Once again McBride – this time with the captaincy – and McLoughlin were on hand to lead the Irish side into battle. But a battle never eventuated as All Black fullback Joe Karam scored 15 points (a try, a conversion and three penalty goals) in a one-sided 15-6 win.

McBride would never play another test against the All Blacks. However, he would turn out for two highly rated Barbarians teams. In 1973 he joined a number of his teammates from the 1971 Lions' tour of New Zealand in the Barbarians side that defeated the All Blacks 23-11 in Cardiff and in 1974 he captained the Barbarians side which held Andy Leslie's All Blacks to a 13-all draw.

The most memorable of these two Barbarians games was, of course, the famous 1973 Cardiff encounter. It wasn't a game where a lock forward was going to make an impression as backs like Phil Bennett, Gareth Edwards, JPR Williams and Grant Batty took the game to a new level of excitement.

"It was a marvellous occasion," says McBride. "People have talked about that game being the best game of rugby ever played. I don't know if I contributed anything. All I had to do was win the ball in the lineout and give it to the backs and then try my hardest to keep up with them. It was end-to-end stuff, not the hard confrontational battles that I enjoyed. But, I couldn't complain... I had the best seat in the house."

WILLIE JOHN McBRIDE AGAINST THE ALL BLACKS

Date	For	Venue	Result	Score	Points
7-12-63	Ireland	Dublin	lost	5-6	
25-1-64	Ulster	Belfast	lost	5-24	
6-8-66	British Isles	Wellington	lost	12-16	
27-8-66	British Isles	Christchurch	lost	6-19	
10-9-66	British Isles	Auckland	lost	11-24	
26-6-71	British Isles	Dunedin	won	9-3	
10-7-71	British Isles	Christchurch	lost	12-22	
31-7-71	British Isles	Wellington	won	13-3	
14-8-71	British Isles	Auckland	drew	14-14	
18-11-72	Ulster	Belfast	lost	6-19	
20-1-73	Ireland	Dublin	drew	10-10	
27-1-73	Barbarians	Cardiff	won	23-11	
16-11-74	Ulster	Belfast	lost	15-30	
23-11-74	Ireland	Dublin	lost	6-15	
30-11-74	Barbarians	London	drew	13-13	

TEST MATCH CAREER

	P	W	L	D	T	C	P	Dg	Pts
vs All Blacks	10	2	6	2	-	-	-	-	-
All Tests	80	32	35	13	1	-	-	-	4

Brian Moore

"He's from the old-fashioned school of hookers, but it's his mouth which is the most obvious feature of his game"

Sean Fitzpatrick
(**Fronting Up,** 1994)

Date of birth: 11-1-1962
Born at: Birmingham, England
Position: Hooker
Test matches: 69

PERHAPS it can be put down to something as simple as self belief. Whatever he had, coaches preparing to do battle with the All Blacks would all wish they could have someone like Brian Moore in their ranks. This was a man who in many ways didn't have the right to be as confident as he was. He wasn't the most skilful hooker ever to pull on the No 2 jersey. He wasn't the strongest. He wasn't the fastest. But he had heart. He had desire. He believed in himself.

"You've got to be able to do that," he says. "If you play against the All Blacks and somewhere inside your make-up you don't believe you can beat them, the only sure thing is that you will get beaten. It's as though the All Blacks can smell fear. They can look you in the eye and they know if you are up to it or not. If you are, you've gone a long way to earning their respect. If you're not, they'll sense it. They'll put you under enormous pressure and attack you all day.

"As an opponent of the All Blacks there can be no in-between. You live, or you die."

❧

THE first meeting is always a memorable one. The fact that it was the opening game of the 1991 World Cup against the All Blacks at Twickenham only added to the occasion.

"Take away the fact that it was a World Cup game and it would still have been a massive occasion," says Brian Moore. "There is nothing bigger than playing against the All Blacks. There's a real sense of tradition that surrounds the games England play against teams like Scotland and France but there is something special about playing a side like New Zealand."

Confidence within the England camp going into the World Cup opener against the defending champions was high. They had won the Five Nations championship earlier in the year and were aware, as was the rest of the rugby world, that the 1991 All Blacks were on the slide.

"If the World Cup had fallen two years earlier I don't think any side in the world would have come close to stopping the All Blacks. In that era, with Buck Shelford at the helm, they were unstoppable. But by the time the World Cup rolled around they had begun to struggle a bit. A few of their players were coming to the end of their careers and perhaps were guilty of staying in the team a season or two too long.

"But there was still a healthy respect for them. They were still the All Blacks. They were the defending champions and we knew we would have to play somewhere near our very best just to be competitive. The difference was that we believed we would be. We believed we could win... no question about that."

It's hard to argue with the confidence that Moore and his teammates felt.

In the two tests against the Wallabies the All Blacks had managed only a solitary try, to lock Ian Jones. There was little fluidity to the backline play and for all the criticism from New Zealanders about the state of England's faltering backline, the All Blacks were hardly in a position to rate themselves as any more spectacular.

"Man-for-man we matched up well," says Moore. "Any pressure

we felt was down to the occasion rather than the fact we were playing against the All Blacks."

"The pressure was enormous," says Moore. "It didn't really matter what the press or the public were saying; our own expectations were high so the pressure was there anyway. We honestly thought that we could win the World Cup and the best way to prove it was by going out on day one and beating New Zealand."

As it was, New Zealand, with a try from Michael Jones and a conversion and four penalties from Grant Fox, triumphed 18-12. Moore's All Black education had begun.

"One of England's strengths in the Five Nations championships at the time was our ability to ram home any advantage that we had," he says. "If we were on attack and the opposition gave away a string of penalties you could be sure that we'd kick the goals to win the match. Or if a team had a weakness we'd find it and expose the opposition. But here was a team, not at their peak, that were doing it to us.

"We had our chances to win the game but we didn't take them. The All Black had chances to win the game and they took them. Everything I'd heard about playing the All Blacks was true. They were ruthless and uncompromising. They had done to us what we had been doing to others.

"It didn't help that we froze a bit. Because England hadn't played the All Blacks since 1983 we didn't know what to expect. It took 25 minutes before we realised we could compete with them. It doesn't matter how confident we'd been beforehand, when we ran out there and started playing the test it was as though we were in awe of the them.

"Instead of talking about playing them, there we were on the same pitch as them. You start thinking about all the adjectives people use – fearsome, warrior-like, mighty. Although journos use them because they're convenient and add spice, when you hear them often enough the myth can quickly turn into reality."

The test also signalled the beginning of Moore's rivalry with All Black hooker Sean Fitzpatrick. Both men had similar combative qualities. Neither man was interested in taking a backward step and that meant plenty of "incidents" and just as many verbals.

"Fitzpatrick would have been a good referee," says Moore. "He certainly never stopped chipping away at the refs. He was something special all right because he managed to see every little thing that happened on a rugby field... even when he had his head buried in a scrum! He had an opinion on everything. I didn't need to watch the videos of games I played in against him because he'd already given me a running commentary of what was happening out there. But the fact is, if I was coaching a side he'd be one of the guys I would have wanted in my team. He's one of the great competitors. He was a bit fiery and a bit dirty at times but that isn't necessarily a bad thing. You need someone like that leading from the front and setting the ground rules.

"What made Fitzpatrick great, though, was that you could take away all that peripheral stuff – the constant chit-chat and so on – and you'd be left with a fantastic player. He could scrummage as well as anyone and his work-rate was first class. If there is one thing I can't stand it's players who swan around thinking they own the place but can't back it up with a bit of talent. Fitzy could always do that. He talked the talk, but he walked the walk."

Ironically, England's loss to the All Blacks meant they avoided tournament favourite Australia in the semifinals. Instead, they played Scotland, whom they beat 9-6 before eventually going down to the Wallabies 12-6 in the final.

Before the World Cup final, All Black co-coach John Hart had publicly put his support behind the Australians saying, "God help the game if England wins the World Cup. Australia epitomises what is good about rugby. My criticism of England is that this game is played to run the ball, not just kick and chase."

"I wonder if John Hart would rather have lost in a semifinal or had the chance to win the World Cup by lining up in the final," says Moore. "It was a stupid comment to make. Okay, we didn't play the most expansive game at the tournament but why should we? Surely at a World Cup the whole point is to try and win it. The only way you are going to do that is by playing to your strengths. That's exactly what we did.

"The All Blacks hardly set the tournament alight anyway. It was the sort of comment that when you hear it for the first time you wonder why the person being quoted doesn't get his own house in order first.

The All Blacks of 1991 were hardly the model that the world should be following, were they? They had two coaches who didn't get along and players who didn't get along either with themselves or the public. They were an aloof lot... it was quite obvious they had little time for anyone not directly associated with the team.

"It was the only All Black team I can remember that thrived on unpleasant mouthing off. Richard Loe, for instance, would come out with things like *I thought you'd be better than this* or *I thought you would be able to push harder than this*. It gives me great satisfaction to know that while we were playing the World Cup final the New Zealanders were licking their semifinal wounds."

OUT OF THE ASHES... (Part I)

If there was ever a competition run to name the defining moment in rugby in 1993 it would be a no-brainer. The choice is easy – although a little more difficult for the All Blacks of the time to admit to.

The day came two days after Christmas at London's Twickenham. The All Blacks, fresh from a 51-15 rout of Scotland, rolled into London with the swagger that was associated with the great New Zealand teams of the past.

Since New Zealand's World Cup exit at the hands of Australia in 1991 there had been many changes to All Black rugby. Laurie Mains was now the coach and the old guard were out of his team. Experienced players like Sean Fitzpatrick, Grant Fox, Ian Jones and Zinzan Brooke and a new brigade of brash youngsters like Robin Brooke, Arran Pene, Jamie Joseph, John Timu, Marc Ellis and Jeff Wilson were now in starring roles.

The England test was supposed to be a formality. Instead, the image beamed across the rugby world was that of England's captain Will Carling being hoisted high by England's fans as they carried him off the famous Twickenham turf. England had beaten the All Blacks 15-9.

"What's it like to beat the All Blacks?" says Brian Moore. "It was bloody brilliant! Beating the All Blacks provides you with the greatest thrill in rugby. The All Blacks are what every team playing rugby measures themselves against. You can beat Scotland or even Australia and walk off the park feeling very satisfied. But it doesn't compare to beating New Zealand. That's a very special feeling. It's like taking on the master.

"Don't get me wrong... it's not as though we were in awe of the All Blacks and had accomplished the impossible dream or anything like that. It's just that wins against them don't come around too often. If you are lucky enough to be on a side that beats them you know you have to cherish it because it's a rare thing for any team to beat them consecutively."

The victory was even more special to Moore and his teammates as 13 of the England team that day had been on the unsuccessful British Lions tour to New Zealand earlier that year.

"If nothing else, we'd come away from New Zealand as better players," says Moore. "When you tour New Zealand and you play the Otagos, the Wellingtons and the Aucklands, you have no choice but to learn as you go. You can't help but expand your knowledge of the game when you are playing so many tough games. You learn as much about the game as you do about yourself.

"Any tour of New Zealand is extremely demanding, both mentally and physically, because the pressure is never off. There are simply no easy games on a tour in New Zealand. Every provincial team you play is desperate to beat you and many of them had the players to make that a real possibility. When you are playing in those circumstances – knowing you have to perform to your highest level each week – you have two choices. You can either buckle under the pressure or you can thrive."

The adversity for the Lions started even before the first test in Christchurch when they were beaten by Otago 37-24. "If any of us were under any illusions about how tough it would be, that game would have put them right," says Moore. "We were a proud group of players. We took no joy at all out of the fact that we'd been beaten by a provincial side. It stung a few of the lads. You could call it a wake-up call but in many respects it was a reality check. This was going to be one of the hardest tours any of us had undertaken... that was clear from day one."

Moore missed selection for the first test when Lions coach Ian McGeechan – a former Scottish international – selected Scotland's Kevin Milne ahead of him. But after the test was lost 20-18, Moore,

England lock Martin Johnson and Welsh centre Scott Gibbs were brought into the team for the second test at Wellington's Athletic Park.

In spite of the first test being lost there was no self-doubt creeping into the touring party. The *We wuz robbed* signs were put up by Lions management as soon as the first test was lost. They were furious at Australian referee Brian Kinsey, who had allowed a first-minute try to Frank Bunce in controversial circumstances as well as awarding a 77th-minute penalty against their No 8 Dean Richards, which gave Grant Fox the chance to win the game for the All Blacks.

"We were gutted," says Moore. "If the referee had got just one of those decisions right we would have been 1-0 up in the series. As it was, our backs were up against the wall. If we'd lost in Wellington the whole tour would have been a complete disaster."

Determination to turn the negative of Lancaster Park into a positive at Athletic Park fuelled the Lions in the build-up to the second test. They were determined to prove they were good enough to beat the All Blacks. Then the All Black selectors seemed to help the Lions' cause when they made a number of changes to their test team despite being 1-0 in the series. John Kirwan was restored to the wing with Eroni Clarke replacing Walter Little at second five-eighth. Halfback Ant Strachan was replaced by Jon Preston and lock Ian Jones was replaced by Mark Cooksley.

The locking move was a disaster. Martin Johnson and Martin Bayfield dominated in the first half, winning 14 lineouts, doubling the effort of Cooksley and Robin Brooke. At halftime Laurie Mains restored Ian Jones to the fray but the British Lion had already bolted. The Lions had answered an Eroni Clarke try and Grant Fox conversion with three penalties from captain Gavin Hastings to lead 9-7 at the break. That lead was eventually stretched to 20-7 after a try from Rory Underwood midway through the half broke the game open.

"There was plenty of resolve in the Lions that day," says Moore. "To keep the All Blacks scoreless in the second half was a bonus. We had played the way that we knew we could and we'd hung on for the win that we should have had in Christchurch. It was a marvellous experience. There was a mixture of relief and absolute joy when the final whistle went. The most important thing was that we'd kept the series alive."

The New Zealand selectors reacted to the loss in Wellington by making three changes. Ian Jones was restored to the starting line-up, while Lee Stensness replaced Eroni Clarke and Zinzan Brooke was dropped to make way for Arran Pene.

The All Black management had every right to be concerned early in the match when the Lions dominated territorially. Luckily for New Zealand, Gavin Hastings was having an ordinary day with his kicking boot. He missed his first two penalty attempts before raising the flags in the 15th minute – the same time that Jones limped from the field to be replaced by Cooksley. In the 23rd minute the Lions had stretched the lead to 10-0 when centre Scott Gibbs took advantage of an error from Frank Bunce.

"There is never a lot of joy thinking back to that test," says Moore. "We certainly had the better of the early stages of the game. I don't know that we relaxed when we went 10-0 up... I think it was just a case of the All Blacks lifting their game. Slowly but surely they chipped away at us. Our lead got smaller, then they were in front. I remember sensing their confidence was growing. They started to believe in themselves again; they started to play the way you expect All Black teams to play. Once they'd regained that confidence we were gone. In the end, on the scoreboard at least, it was a bit of a hammering."

Moore was criticised in New Zealand for bypassing the on-field presentation and lap of honour by the Lions. But Moore – someone who feels defeat deeply – simply needed time to grieve.

"In the last few years I have watched the England team do a lap of honour after losing a test to the All Blacks, and I've seen coach Clive Woodward thumping his fist in the air when England have scored a try against Italy! When we lost the third test at Eden Park I wanted to get out of sight. I wasn't proud we'd lost a series. I didn't want to go around waving to the crowd because if I'd been in the stands I would have thought the Lions looked stupid carrying on like that.

"The reason All Black rugby is so good is because they *feel* their defeats. It was no coincidence Craig Dowd was the most outstanding player on the pitch for New Zealand when they beat England in their pool game at the 1999 World Cup. He was driven by the desire to avenge a defeat to England seven years earlier. I was the same. I hated losing. It's a very un-English attitude. The biggest problem with our game is that too many people settle for just being involved. For me, that was never good enough. If you aren't out there to win, then you should just fuck off and go play cricket."

Sean Fitzpatrick, now the captain of the All Blacks, played a key role in the All Black turnaround. After Frank Bunce had made up for his earlier error by scoring New Zealand's first try, it was Fitzpatrick's try that lifted All Black spirits as well as helping New Zealand to a 14-10 halftime lead.

"Fitzpatrick had come a long way since our first meeting at test level in 1991," says Moore. "He seemed to thrive in the captaincy. He had always been a natural leader but he had probably not been allowed to lead in that 1991 side. But this was definitely Fitzpatrick's team. He was the boss out there. He was as hard and uncompromising as ever but he had the ability to switch into the leadership role with ease. It would be too easy to say that he led by example. He was always encouraging the lads around him – especially the younger ones.

"But I always had the feeling Fitzy was a bully on the field. If you gave an inch, or showed weakness, he'd go for your throat. He wasn't a playground bully. He'd respect you if you stood square to him. There were times when I hated him, but I've mellowed a bit. I may not have liked Fitzy very much, but I respected him as a player... I always will."

The test, and with it the series, was effectively over in the 66th minute when Jon Preston scored New Zealand's third try and helped secure the final 30-13 scoreline. For the All Blacks it was a sign that Laurie Mains' young team was coming of age. For the Lions, and in particular the 16 Englishmen in the squad, it provided ample motivation for a test at Twickenham six months later.

"Obviously, it wasn't England that lost at Eden Park that day," says Moore, "but by the time the test at Twickenham came around revenge was definitely on our minds. There is no question in my mind that we would have won the series if it hadn't been for the poor refereeing in the first test. Okay, we hadn't been good enough to bounce back from it, but we knew that the All Blacks weren't unbeatable. The Lions had proved that. Now it was England's turn to prove it."

With the Lions' series undoubtably the priority for Mains and his coaching staff in 1993, the New Zealand selectors used their 13-match tour of Scotland and England to blood some new players. Two notable absentees were winger John Kirwan and first five-eighth Grant Fox. For the tour's first test against Scotland, Jeff Wilson and Marc Ellis were given the responsibility of filling in for the All Black legends and initially they did remarkably well.

In beating Scotland 51-15 the All Blacks recorded a record-winning margin against the Scots. Jeff Wilson, who would end the century as arguably the All Blacks' greatest-ever winger, scored an astonishing three tries on his debut – becoming only the third All Black, behind Frank Mitchinson (1907) and Tom Lynch (1913), to achieve that milestone. Ellis had a game from the top-drawer as well as he thrived outside Otago halfback Stu Forster (also on debut) and chimed in with two tries of his own.

It had been a masterful performance by New Zealand and a similar effort was widely expected against England.

England went into the test with two new caps – fullback Jonathan Callard and halfback Kyran Bracken. The rest of the side were stacked full of experience. Captain Will Carling was in charge of a team that boasted names like Brian Moore, Martin Johnson, Jason Leonard, Ben Clarke, Dean Richards, Rob Andrew, Rory Underwood and Jeremy Guscott – all of whom had starred for the Lions.

New Zealand's chances weren't helped when Matthew Cooper, injured against Scotland, was ruled out of the Twickenham test. He had won his place in the touring side for his goalkicking as much as anything and, with Cooper sidelined, the goalkicking duties fell to 20-year-old Wilson.

Wilson had a shocker, missing three first-half penalty attempts as the All Blacks limped into halftime down 0-6. In the second half he managed to find the target three times but it was too little too late as Callard, with four penalties, and Andrew, a dropped goal, combined to help England to the 15-9 win.

"We had done it," says Moore. "It was a feeling of absolute elation. There is pressure in every test you play and on that day it got to the All Blacks more than it did to England. We coped with everything they threw at us. It was a fantastic feeling.

"The remarkable thing about the day was the response of the fans. They were ecstatic. You realise very quickly when you win a test against the mighty All Blacks that it affects everyone. It wasn't just about the England lads getting a bit of revenge. This was the country's victory. Everyone was touched by it. That's what beating the All Blacks can do. We were heroes. It was as though we were on top of the rugby world."

OUT OF THE ASHES... (Part II)

It's ironic that the Lions' defeat in New Zealand in 1993 provided the motivation for England's shock win against the All Blacks later that year because it would be the All Blacks who would draw on that black day at Twickenham for stimulus two years later when the two sides met again at the 1995 World Cup.

Mention that game to any Englishman – be it a player or a spectator – and they noticeably shrink in stature. Brian Moore is no different.

"It's a day I'd rather forget," he says. "The sort of day that you wish had never happened... the sort of day you wish *everyone* would forget."

It was, of course, the day that Jonah Lomu launched himself on the world. He'd already impressed with tries in the earlier rounds against Ireland and Scotland. But those games were his coming-out party; the semifinal against England was his coronation.

England had qualified for the semifinal with a quarter-final win against defending champions Australia. It was the sort of win that should have filled them with an undentable confidence but there's no question Jonah Lomu had some of Moore's teammates spooked.

"I'm sure some of the lads didn't like the idea of having to tackle him," says Moore. "I don't suppose many people would. But if you are going into the semifinal of a World Cup you have to have the frame of mind where you not only think you can take him down but you are looking forward to stopping him. It's an obvious thing to say but how can you expect to beat a team like the All Blacks unless you are totally convinced you can.

"In any sport, against any good side, you need to be able to match their confidence. You can't go out there worried about a certain player. You shouldn't even worry about the opposition. But some of our lads were obviously worried. They tried to be confident but there was an uneasy feeling within the team before the game. Something was missing. The lads were saying the right things but deep down you wondered whether they meant it."

Within two minutes of the kick-off Lomu had scored his first try when he crashed through attempted tackles by Tony Underwood and Mike Catt. A minute later Josh Kronfeld scored and it was 12-0. In the 25th minute Lomu scored again... 25-0.

At halftime, with the score 25-3 and the English shell-shocked, England's captain tried to rally his troops. *Heads up lads. Make sure we're the first to score in this half. Chip away at them. We've beaten them before, we can beat them again.* Whether Will Carling believed what he was saying is irrelevant because, one minute into the half, Lomu scored his third try. Nine minutes later it was Graeme Bachop's turn. Rory Underwood and Carling launched something of a comeback by scoring tries but Lomu, between times, grabbed his fourth and the match ended with a scoreline of 45-29.

It would be Moore's last game against the All Blacks. Indeed, his test career ended a few days later when he played in the third/fourth play-off against France, all of his World Cup-winning dreams shattered.

"I remember feeling empty," he says. "Gutted, I guess. This was Jonah Lomu at his best. This was All Black rugby at its best. It's a sad memory."

BRIAN MOORE AGAINST THE ALL BLACKS

Date	For	Venue	Result	Score	Points
3-10-91	England	London	lost	12-18	
26-6-93	British Isles	Wellington	won	20-7	
3-7-93	British Isles	Auckland	lost	13-30	
23-10-93	London SE Div	London	lost	12-39	
27-11-93	England	London	won	15-9	
18-6-95	England	Cape Town	lost	29-45	

TEST MATCH CAREER

	P	W	L	D	T	C	P	Dg	Pts
vs All Blacks	5	2	3	-	-	-	-	-	-
All Tests	69	48	20	1	1	-	-	-	4

François Pienaar

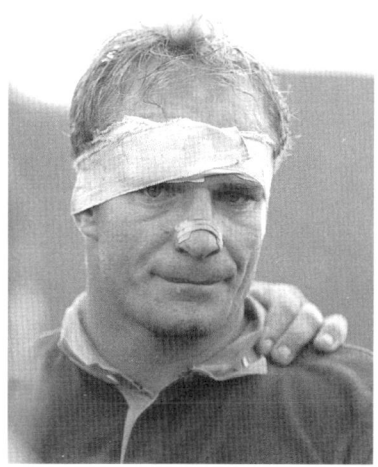

Date of birth: 2-1-1967
Born at: Port Elizabeth,
     South Africa
Position: Flanker
Test matches: 29

"I was taken aback when he was dropped as captain of the team because he is the man who led our team to that unprecedented victory against the All Blacks in the final of the World Cup. It had been a victory for Africa as a whole and it's a day that will always be remembered for the coming of age of the Rainbow Nation – that's how important that victory was"

Nelson Mandela

HE cannot help himself. He should be one of the most content men in rugby but the guilt is the lingering kind. When he hears words like loyalty **and** allegiance **he shudders. And then he shudders again. And again. He doesn't stop until the realisation that you can't turn back time hits.**

He cannot stop himself. He knows that what is done is done. He made a mistake and he must forgive himself. But François Pienaar is a complicated man. Wrongs must be made into right. His father taught him that.

He cannot understand himself. Given the same situation today he wouldn't be silent. He would stand up and be heard. He would be the captain that he became a year after the incident. He's embarrassed when he thinks of his lack of leadership. *I thought I was a better captain than that.*

Pienaar wrote himself into rugby folklore when he captained the Springboks to their World Cup victory in 1995. It was one of those glorious moments in sport which will forever be remembered as much for the rebirth of a country's spirit as it was for the dramatic finale to a thrilling final. It was, without a doubt, South Africa's day. Springbok coach Kitch Christie's quote "One team, one country" will forever be remembered as the rallying cry of a home side desperate to garner support from all of South Africa's population groups and to use the world's biggest rugby stage to showpiece a nation rebuilding itself.

It would seem ridiculous to suggest that any other moment in the life and rugby times of François Pienaar could have been more of a defining moment. But talk to Pienaar and you face a man who is still struggling with a decision he made a year before he was to lift the William Webb Ellis trophy. It was an incident where he learned more about himself than anything he learned when he accepted the adulation of a nation as the captain of the newly crowned world champions.

The episode unfolded during the Springboks' 1994 tour to New Zealand. During the second test at Athletic Park the rugby world was sent into uproar when television cameras zoomed in on Springbok prop Johan le Roux and Sean Fitzpatrick. As play moved on up the field the two were involved in something akin to a wrestling match when le Roux bit Fitzpatrick's ear. It was a deliberate act and when le Roux fronted to the judiciary he was banned from all rugby for 18 months. He was also sent home by the South African management – something Pienaar regrets.

"I wasn't experienced enough to handle that incident," says Pienaar, who had broken into the Springbok side only 12 months earlier. "I think I let Johan down; I didn't stand behind him and back him. Everyone slated him and said he was a disgrace and I said nothing. I didn't go out of my way to support him. None of us did.

"On the day he had to face the tribunal the rest of us were on a harbour cruise. The guy was left alone. He even had to find his own lawyer.

"I should have backed him but I didn't. When the management said he had to go home I didn't say he should stay. All those things I should have done differently. You don't abandon your players like that. It was his hour of need and we turned our backs on him. It was unforgivable.

"I'm not saying that he shouldn't have been punished... make no mistake about that. But the punishment he received did not fit the crime. I have looked at the video of the incident many times and there is no doubt that there was some provocation going on. Sean Fitzpatrick was not an angel. He had a part to play in all this.

"To ban Johan le Roux for 18 months was very harsh. Yes, you don't want players biting other players. Yes, he shouldn't have done it. Yes, he should have been punished. But 18 months? That was a serious amount of time. In the modern day if you smash a guy in the face with a good punch you get two weeks. The punishment he received effectively ended his career. I will never forgive myself for my lack of action.

"I have learned to judge myself by my own standards. It's too easy when you are a high-profile sportsman to believe all the good things that are written about you. People say I was a great captain. But they only say that because I captained the team which won the World Cup. If we hadn't won the final I wonder if people would still be saying I was a great player? It can be very superficial. When I look back at my career and I judge myself I know that in 1994 I let myself and one of my teammates down. It's not the easiest thing to live with."

꩜

THE All Blacks were a few long steps from their second World Cup triumph and the Springboks were a few short steps from the rugby graveyard. The South Africans had just lost a three-test series against New Zealand and the prospect of hosting the 1995 World Cup the following year all of a sudden didn't look like the opportunity they had once hoped it would be.

It had been the first Springbok tour to New Zealand since 1981. South Africa's politics, and in particular its apartheid policies, meant that there had been no rugby contact between the two countries until 1992 when the All Blacks played a one-off test at Johannesburg's Ellis Park.

"The excitement level within the squad was sensational," says Pienaar. "All of us at some stage or another had dreamed about playing against the mighty All Blacks and there we were, on our way to New Zealand to do battle with our great rivals. I felt so very privileged to be involved in the tour. It was an extremely daunting exercise but I couldn't wait to get there. I couldn't wait to be a part of the renewal of the rivalry."

To understand the excitement on the eve of the tour, it must first be understood that no one in the Springbok squad could ever be sure that they would get the chance to play international rugby. Pienaar's experience was typical.

"My first real memory of the All Blacks was watching the 1981 tour on television," he says. "It coincided with the time that I started to think about politics. I grew up in a South Africa where the government of the day, the government which we all supported, was spreading propaganda in the newspapers so you never really knew the full extent of what was going on in South Africa.

"I remember watching the Springboks' game against Waikato in Hamilton and seeing all the demonstrators on the field. I asked my father why it was happening and he couldn't really give me the answers that I was after. My father was a working-class man and he would just say that it was bloody politics. It wasn't until I got to university that I began to understand what was happening in South Africa. The events of 1981 began to make sense.

"Having learned a little about the politics of the white government it became clear to me that the only rugby I would play would be local. The thought that isolation would one day end and we would get the chance to play against teams like the All Blacks was fantasy stuff. Our international rugby was the Currie Cup. That was the highest thing that we could aim for."

Pienaar's passion for rugby was fuelled by the 1986 visit of the rebel New Zealand Cavaliers side. Made up of every All Black of the time – with the exception of only John Kirwan and David Kirk – the Cavaliers played four matches against the Springboks.

"I was glued to the series," says Pienaar. "It was an amazing event for us. To see men like Murray Mexted, Mark Shaw and Jock Hobbs... it was magic. They had instant respect everywhere they went. Of course, the South African public wanted to see them get beaten, but there was an underlying feeling of respect. These great men had risked their international careers to take on the Springboks."

When the barriers of isolation were eventually broken down in 1992, Pienaar's delight at the prospect of playing international rugby turned sour when he was overlooked by coach John Williams. It was a devastating blow for the schoolboy star who had gone on to be selected for South Africa at every age-group level. In fact, he wasn't even deemed good enough to make the Junior Springbok team which toured Namibia.

"I figured that my standard of play was just not good enough," he says. "I actually thought that my chance had gone. I thought my Springbok dream was over before it even started."

A top-draw domestic year for Transvaal in 1993, however, saw him force his way into the South African team and a test series in Australia. And while the chance to play against the Wallabies was not something to be dismissed, it did not compare to the journey he was about to undertake to New Zealand.

"Touring New Zealand is the ultimate tour. There have been so many great series between the two countries. You hear stories about the great Springbok team of 1949, the brutal series in New Zealand in 1956 and the revenge of 1970. There is so much history. Now I had a chance to play my part in the greatest rivalry in rugby."

As the Springboks began their tour, the All Blacks were in the process of losing a home series against the French. The All Blacks, with a young Jonah Lomu playing his first tests, looked feeble as they went down 22-8 in Christchurch and 23-20 in Auckland. In contrast, the Springboks had impressed in their tour games, registering wins against King Country, Counties, Wellington and a Hanan Shield Districts team before the first test in Dunedin.

"When we looked at the videotapes of their games against the French it was hard not to think that we could beat them," says Pienaar. "They hadn't played very well at all and we really rated our chances of upsetting them. But in hindsight we didn't have very much experience of playing against the All Blacks. There had been only one test between the two countries since 1981 and we were probably a little naive to think that we could march into New Zealand and beat the All Blacks. It was possible, but I'm not so sure that we realised how tough it would be to play against the All Blacks in New Zealand."

Pienaar had been given an early lesson in the toughness of New Zealand rugby when he was concussed during the Boks' 36-26 win against Wellington. The injury meant that he would miss the Carisbrook test.

Laurie Mains had reacted to the defeats at the hands of France by making three changes to his test team. Fullback Shane Howarth was brought into the team to allow John Timu to play on the left wing, replacing Jonah Lomu, while second-five Matthew Cooper was dropped for Alama Ieremia and Graeme Bachop took over at halfback from Stu Forster. The Springboks, with the exception of Pienaar, were at full strength. And while they were still something of an unknown quantity, it was no surprise when they started confidently, taking an early 3-0 lead through the boot of fullback Andre Joubert. If there was a difference between the two sides it was discipline – or a lack of it from the South Africans. While the try-scoring honours were shared – Kirwan dotting down for the All Blacks and flanker Rudolf Straeuli scoring for the Boks – it would be Howarth's five penalty goals that would provide the bulk of New Zealand's points in the 22-14 win.

"We could have won the test, perhaps should have won the test," says Pienaar. "But we lacked discipline. It was frustrating watching from the stands and seeing the guys play into the All Blacks' hands. It was immediately obvious to me that if you are going to beat New Zealand you have to play a very disciplined style of rugby."

The All Blacks clinched the series with a 13-9 victory at Athletic Park. While the scoreline was close it did not reflect the one-sidedness of the test. The All Blacks totally dominated the forward battle with Pienaar's presence making little difference to the South African effort up front.

As with every South African series loss against the All Blacks, it didn't take long before the supporters and media were calling for coach Ian McIntosh's head (he would be sacked on the team's return to the republic). Failure was not acceptable at the best of times, let alone against the All Blacks. The criticism from home and the le Roux incident ensured the Springbok team that fronted at Eden Park for the third test were a fired-up one.

"It had been a hard tour," says Pienaar. "There had been a lot of negative press in New Zealand after the Johan le Roux incident and after a while it began to affect the guys. We could sense that there was a strong anti-Springbok feeling.

"As well as that we had been unhappy with the way the tour had gone. We were outplayed in the second test and we knew that we would be a laughing stock if we were unable to get out of Auckland without another loss. The pressure was building up and the guys were feeling it. It wasn't the ideal build-up to such an important game but we couldn't really have expected anything else. We were looking a 3-0 series defeat in the face and it was up to us to stop it from happening."

Pienaar's men responded to the challenge with winger Gavin Johnson and centre Brendan Venter scoring the test's only tries. The Springboks looked on course for victory but in the 71st minute, when they were leading 18-15, Venter threw a punch at one of the All Blacks and Shane Howarth stepped up to kick his sixth penalty of the day and secure an 18-18 draw.

"It was very difficult to go back to South Africa and look people in the eye with any real conviction after that," says Pienaar. "Results-wise it had been a disastrous tour. We'd lost the series 2-0 and we had become the first South African side in 73 years of contests between the All Blacks and the Springboks which had failed to win a test in a series. Those were pretty dark days."

Ironically, it was out of the ashes of the 1994 tour that crucial lessons, which would be drawn on before the 1995 World Cup final against New Zealand, were learned. Says Pienaar: "It is not an over-exaggeration to say that we would not have won the World Cup if it hadn't been for the things we gained on tour in New Zealand. The biggest asset we came out of New Zealand with was experience. The All Blacks – Sean Fitzpatrick in particular – were experts at getting under your skin. Whether they were pushing you in the back off the ball or holding you down on the ground after the ball had been cleared from a ruck they had mastered their own form of gamesmanship.

"We let it get to us. We weren't as focused as we should have been. We were too easily distracted. The All Blacks did those sorts of things to try and switch our focus away from our game plan... and it worked. When the World Cup came along we knew that if we played against the All Blacks we would have to guard against it happening again.

"The shining light from the 1994 tour was that, in the two tests we lost, we'd only gone down by eight and four points. It wasn't as though we'd been thrashed. We knew that we would have to take every opportunity that came our way because a victory was only a penalty or a dropped goal away. Discipline was going to be the key for us. If we could ignore the antics of a Fitzpatrick, then we would have a chance."

Pienaar and the rest of South Africa got their chance for the greatest revenge possible when both sides qualified for the World Cup final. The Boks had got there by way of pool victories against Australia (27-18), Romania (21-8) and Canada (20-0), a quarter-final win against Manu Samoa (42-14) and a semifinal triumph against France (19-15). The All Blacks had cruised through to the final with group wins against Ireland (43-19), Wales (34-9) and Japan (145-17) before accounting for Scotland (48-30) in the quarter-finals and humiliating England (45-29) in the semifinal.

Laurie Mains' All Blacks went into the final as hot favourites. Not only did they boast the more impressive record but they had a winger by the name of Jonah Lomu – the individual star of the tournament. Lomu had been in devastating form right from the outset of the World Cup when scoring two tries against Ireland. There was another try in the win against Scotland before he claimed four in the win against England.

"The guy was a phenomenon," says Pienaar. "It was hard to believe that he was the same guy we had watched play against France a year earlier. Then he looked out of his depth at test level. But by the time of the final he was the best thing going around in rugby."

Despite the danger that Lomu presented, the Springbok players were hoping the All Blacks would join them in the final. "We were wary of the All Blacks because they had had such a great tournament. Australia had come to the World Cup as the favourites but it wasn't long before the All Blacks were the team to beat. Maybe the final would have been easier to win if England had been there but I think that, to a man, we wanted to play New Zealand. Tradition demanded it. It was the dream final. You couldn't have written a more perfect script. The old rivals going head-to-head for the greatest prize of all."

The Springboks knew the first thing they would have to confront in the build-up to the final was Jonah-mania. How were they going to do what Ireland, Scotland and England had failed to do?

"We were wary of Lomu," says Pienaar. "Kitch Christie refused to talk too much about Jonah. I guess he didn't want to remind us of how good he was! When we asked him how we were going to stop Lomu he just shrugged his shoulders and said James would look after him.

"We decided that we couldn't pay too much attention to him because there were 14 other superstars in that side that we had to keep an eye on. The only alteration we made to combat him was to deny him outside space. All the tries he had scored in the World Cup were scored on the outside going in to the corner. If you allow a guy with that pace and that power to get on the outside of you you're asking for trouble. We decided to place winger James Small outside of Lomu the whole time to try and force him infield towards the cover defence. We did our best to stick to the game plan but, once the game started, every time time Lomu touched the ball everyone wanted to have a go and smash him. We were like a team on the hunt. Everyone wanted to dig in and help James Small out as much as possible."

The gang-tackling on Lomu came after a significant moment during the pre-game haka when the unity within the South African team was plain for all to see. During the haka, Lomu had sought out Small. As Lomu inched towards the Springbok winger, South African lock Kobus Wiese stepped in front of Small. "It was a unplanned gesture of solidarity," says Pienaar. "Kobus was basically saying *If you want to go through James you are going to have to go through me first.*"

On the morning of the final Pienaar reminded his charges of the lessons that were learned in New Zealand the previous year. "I told them that we had to mimic the All Blacks' gamesmanship. We had to do to them what they had done to us. If we were walking past them we had to make sure we gave them a shove in the shoulder. If we had a chance to hold them on the ground, we had to do that too. The All Blacks needed a dose of their own medicine. We needed to try and get inside their heads. We needed to try and get them thinking about anything but their game plan. We had to challenge and threaten their status. We had to let them know that we had matured since our last meeting."

When the All Blacks walked out onto Ellis Park they were greeted by 62,000 partisan Springbok fans. The presence of President Nelson Mandela had the crowd in raptures. Mandela was an inspirational figure during the World Cup. His public support of the Springboks – he wore a Springbok jersey with Pienaar's No 6 on the back of it to the final – ensured that millions of black South Africans stood firm in their support of a team which for so long were an extension of white supremacy in the republic. The emotion was at such a fever pitch that Pienaar decided not to sing the national anthem because he feared he would burst into tears.

"I was very lucky that once we were out on the field I didn't have to deliver any profound words to the team," says Pienaar. "If I'd needed to I don't know that I would have been able to because the occasion was such an overwhelming one. The message I gave to the team was a simple one. *Look around. Listen to the people singing for us. Just play for them and we will win the World Cup.*

"Of course there were no guarantees that we would win. The fact remained that we had to get by the best team in the tournament. The key was that we knew what we had to do. The message had been delivered throughout the week – it was to take them on at their own game . . ."

Once Ed Morrison signalled for the kick-off it didn't take long for the All Blacks to begin their onslaught. Within minutes of the first whistle, they were three points up, Andrew Mehrtens beginning the first of his damaging attacks with the boot by landing a penalty goal.

But the threat of Jonah Lomu on the wing seemed to have been neutralised, the big man cut down to size on every movement by the likes of Joost van der Westhuizen and Os du Randt.

With the score at 6-3 after an exchange of penalties, there came what many argue was the turning point in the game. South Africa's forwards seemed to push Ruben Kruger over the All Black line for a try but referee Morrison ruled for a scrum. *Held up!*

"Other Springbok teams that I had been involved with would have lost their concentration at that moment," says Pienaar. "But this time, the guys just stayed focused. I knew then that the All Blacks would have to play to their absolute peak to defeat us."

After two more Stransky penalties had given the Springboks a 9-6 halftime lead, the second half started with relentless All Black attacks, their dominance growing with each play. But with each swipe at the green-and-gold, the home side would come back with a seemingly endless supply of defence.

In the 55th minute Mehrtens levelled the scores with his third penalty, the final scoring act of regular time.

The first half of extra time saw Mehrtens once again putting the All Blacks ahead with a penalty goal from inside the Boks' half. But shortly afterwards Stransky again came to the fore with a penalty that found its mark and levelled the scores at 12-12.

The Boks stood to lose should the game be drawn. Based on the IRB rules, should there be no outright winner at the final whistle, the side with the most tries scored would be victorious. As neither side had scored a try, the next step said that the country with fewer players sent off in the duration of the competition would then win. The Springboks found themselves at the wrong end of this rule after their game at the Boet Erasmus stadium against Canada, where James Dalton had received his marching orders.

All this became irrelevant when, in the third minute of the second half of extra time, Stransky collected the ball from van der Westhuizen and drop kicked it high over the bar – the goal taking the score to 15-12. Seven minutes later the game was over. South Africa were world champions.

"It was incredible," says Pienaar. "I remember just dropping to my knees. *We've won. We've won.* It's impossible to describe what I was feeling. One by one my teammates joined me. Each player fell to his knees. I asked Chester Williams to say a prayer of thanks.

There was absolute bedlam in the stadium. The emotions just poured out of all of us. It was an experience beyond anything that I'd imagined."

As the Springboks paraded around Ellis Park with the World Cup, the seeds were already being sown within the All Black camp for revenge of their own in the three-test series in the republic the following year. That they would be successful was a credit to the resolve of men like Sean Fitzpatrick and Zinzan Brooke.

Says Pienaar: "My name came to the fore only because we won the World Cup. I would never place myself in the same class as players like Zinzan and Sean. Zinzan played 58 tests. Sean played 92. That's incredible. Those guys are legends. As an opponent, you show your respect for them by playing your absolute best against them. It's players like them who are responsible for the rivalry between New Zealand and South Africa continuing to be so strong. They may have retired now, but the memories of what they achieved will live on for New Zealanders just as our World Cup win will never be forgotten in South Africa."

Another memory that will live on in South Africa is Laurie Mains' claims that his All Black side was poisoned two days before the final. Mains, who hired a private investigator to look into the goings-on at the All Blacks' hotel, tracked down a waitress named Suzie who was dismissed by hotel management – presumably for her role in the controversy.

But Pienaar has no time for Mains' theory. "I don't believe it for a second," he says. "If something like that had happened to my team I would not rest until it was proven without reasonable doubt that such an event took place. As far as I know nothing has ever been proven. It surprised me when I first heard about it because the All Blacks didn't start talking about it until about a week after the final. Why would they have done that? Again, if it had happened to the Springboks, I would have made sure everyone knew about it as soon as it happened. I would have demanded the investigation begin immediately. Neither of those things happened. It's just another myth to add to the history and traditions of games between South Africa and New Zealand... nothing more, nothing less."

THE ALL BLACKS HAD THE LAST LAUGH

Less the 12 months after winning the World Cup, François Pienaar led his Springboks in the inaugural Tri-Nations tournament against New Zealand and Australia.

Pienaar had been looking forward to the event because his side was only three wins away from passing the All Blacks' record, set between 1965 and 1970, of 17 consecutive test wins. But any enthusiasm he had for the challenge quickly evaporated when Andre Markgraaf was named as the new Springbok coach after Kitch Christie had fallen ill.

It was a mismatch from the start. The pair argued about tactics from the get-go. "I could not agree with his coaching methods during the Tri-Nations series. After all, we had just won the World Cup, so why change a winning formula?"

Pienaar says that as the captain he was bound to follow Markgraaf's instructions to the letter. "But Markgraaf's views were so erratic that the players quickly lost confidence in his approach. His language was atrocious and he abused people, swearing repeatedly. He was not a nice man."

Pienaar was fighting his own battles for popularity after his turnaround on the World Rugby Corporation deal following the World Cup. The bulk of the Wallabies and All Blacks had signed to play for Kerry Packer's new rugby competition but when Pienaar – who originally supported the move – had a change of heart, the proposed deal was scuttled. There was ill-feeling from some senior All Blacks toward him when he arrived in Christchurch for the Tri-Nations. "Some people didn't agree with what I had done but in the end it came down to choice between the traditions of the past or a new beginning. I chose the traditions. I'm convinced it was the right choice. Rugby hasn't exactly suffered in recent years has it?"

It was in those circumstances that the new world champions fronted up to a New Zealand side intent on revenge for the World Cup defeat.

"There is no question that the 1996 All Black side was a better one than the one we played in 1995," says Pienaar. "Now they had a fullback by the name of Christian Cullen. What a player... so fast and lethal. It was another sign of the All Black production line that never stops. It doesn't seem to matter who retires, there's always a replacement."

Despite the behind-the-scene disruptions, South Africa put up a brave fight at Lancaster Park before submitting to the All Blacks 15-11. Fullback Andre Joubert scored the test's only try but Andrew Mehrtens' five penalties were enough to secure the win.

Pienaar's test career would be ended in the return test in Cape Town the following month when he was concussed after attempting a tackle on Sean Fitzpatrick during the All Blacks' 29-18 win. Pienaar is quick to rubbish claims that Fitzpatrick and Zinzan Brooke singled him out for "special treatment" as a payback for his WRC U-turn.

"It's a crazy thing to suggest," says Pienaar. "I had a history of concussion throughout my career. I've watched the video of the match. My head collided with an All Black's knee as I tried to tackle him. It was an accident. I certainly hold no animosity towards any of the All Blacks on the field that day.

"The only upsetting thing was that in my last match against them the All Blacks beat us... I hate it when that happens."

FRANCOIS PIENAAR AGAINST THE ALL BLACKS

Date	For	Venue	Result	Score	Points
23-7-94	South Africa	Wellington	lost	9-13	
6-8-94	South Africa	Auckland	drew	18-18	
24-6-95	South Africa	Johannesburg	won	15-12	
20-7-96	South Africa	Christchurch	lost	11-15	
10-8-96	South Africa	Cape Town	lost	18-29	

TEST MATCH CAREER

	P	W	L	D	T	C	P	Dg	Pts
vs All Blacks	5	1	3	1	-	-	-	-	-
All Tests	29	20	7	2	3	-	-	-	15

Hugo Porta

Date of birth: 11-9-1951
Born at: Buenos Aires, Argentina
Position: First five-eighths
Test matches: 66

"Porta was everything to Argentina, tactician, an astute kicker in field of play, a creator of play, a runner who could make something out of nothing by doing what he was not, sensibly, supposed to do"

Grant Fox
(The Game The Goal, 1992)

WITH Hugo Porta, the conversation always comes back to kicking. You could be talking about the dramatic draws against France in 1977 and New Zealand in 1985, or discussing his hopes and dreams for his country as he starts another day in his Buenos Aires office as Argentina's Minister of Sport. But when the subject is Porta the talk always turns to the wonders he worked with his feet.

In 57 tests for the Pumas, stretching from 1971 to 1990, Porta thrilled rugby fans around the world with his silky running and impressive handling. But it was his boot that saw him enter the record books. He landed 532 points at test level – an effort that in an historic sense puts him in the company of men like Australia's Michael Lynagh and New Zealand's Grant Fox.

There was a time when Hugo Porta, of the film star good looks, was the best flyhalf in the world, a man capable of miracles.

He was not tall, but powerfully built, especially in the waist-thigh area, that part which Cliff Morgan claimed enabled him to play for Wales. Like Morgan, Hugo Porta was a player of great balance. Like Morgan, he was a man with an instinctive eye for a gap, or any semblance of a chance. Unlike Morgan, he was a man who used his strength and acceleration more than his guile and unlike Morgan he had a huge boot. This boot gave Argentine rugby its international status. As a result, unlike Morgan, Porta was inclined to be the man who did it on his own. He was captain and the team's main objective was to give him chances to score.

Probably Hugo Porta's finest rugby hour came in Bloemfontein in 1982. Argentina had never played South Africa at rugby, though they had toured as the Pumas. In fact the first Argentine team to tour abroad went to South Africa in 1965, a team called the Pumas because a journalist, looking for a nickname, decided that the jaguareté on their badge was a puma. Coaching the side was Izak van Heerden, the creative Natal coach. The Pumas came bearing loads of affection and respect for South African rugby, dating back to Barry Heatlie in 1906 and various Junior Springbok and Gazelles teams, for South Africa had taken Argentina under its rugby wing.

The Pumas could not contain their delight in 1965 when they beat the Junior Springboks at Ellis Park. They hugged and lolled about, crying and laughing, loath to leave the field of glory.

Imagine then the delight in Bloemfontein in 1982.

Though the Pumas were not allowed to tour, for political reasons, a conglomerate of nations was formed and called, by some irony, the Jaguars. The team were made up of players from Argentina, Chile, Uruguay, Paraguay, Brazil and Peru – but in playing strength they were the Pumas.

The Jaguars went to South Africa in 1980, 1982 and again, almost entirely on the initiative of Hugo Porta at the prodding of Danie Craven, 1984. In 1980 they played the Springboks in Montevideo and Santiago. In all, the Jaguars, who included two Spanish players in 1984, played eight tests against South Africa. Hugo Porta was captain in all eight. They lost seven, but amid the defeats there was Bloemfontein in 1982.

The first test on that tour had been played in Pretoria and the Springboks broke their record for number of points when they won 62-18. It was all too easy.

The second test was in Bloemfontein. The Springboks gathered, had a grand social time and then went out to finish off the Jaguars. Hugo Porta had other ideas.

That afternoon in the Free State capital, the Springboks scored 12 points, the Jaguars 21. Of the 21 Jaguar points, Porta scored 21. He scored a try, converted it, and kicked four penalty goals and a dropped goal. He scored all his side's points and did so in all ways possible in rugby football. It was a startling performance and perhaps the biggest turnaround international rugby has ever known. And the two matches were only a week apart.

While the Bloemfontein victory may have been the greatest, there were other achievements – 23 points when France beat Argentina 31-27, six kicks against France in 1977 for an 18-all draw and seven kicks (four penalties and three dropped goals) against the All Blacks in 1985 for a 21-all draw. In 1983 his Pumas beat the Wallabies 18-3 in Brisbane and in 1985 France 24-16 in Buenos Aires. In 1987 the Pumas won a home series against the Wallabies.

But it was the draw against the All Blacks in Buenos Aires that is the most fondly remembered by Porta – more so than the game in South Africa because on the occasion in 1985 he had the Puma on his chest.

"To play for Argentina was the greatest thrill," he says. "The only thing better than wearing the blue and white jersey was to wear it against the All Blacks. I think anyone who has ever played rugby wanted to be an All Black. They don't belong to New Zealand anymore. The world has adopted them. They are the world's greatest team."

The All Blacks ventured to Argentina in 1985 after the cancellation of the planned tour to South Africa. They had been to South America once before, in the late 1970s, but this would be the first time the games would be given test status. To appease the players, the squad that was picked to travel to South Africa was reassembled to take on the Argentines. All but three players – captain Andy Dalton, prop John Ashworth and centre Bill

Osborne – took up the offer of the tour.

The All Black side of the day was strong. The forward pack was an uncompromising one dominated by men like Murray Mexted, Mark Shaw, Jock Hobbs, Gary Whetton, Murray Pierce and Gary Knight. The backs were not the most lethal of combinations but in John Kirwan they had one of the best wingers in the world.

"It was so special to play against the All Blacks," says Porta. "It was the biggest challenge. It was extremely daunting for us. It's like the New Zealand soccer team having to play the great Argentina soccer team. It would have been very easy to panic. But in those situations you just think of your country. You feel the Puma jersey on your skin. We are very proud people... we were prepared to put our bodies on the line against the world's greatest players."

Porta, prop Fernando Morel and loose forwards Ernesto Ure and Tomas Petersen were the only survivors from the Argentine team which toured New Zealand in 1979 to turn out on Ferrocarril Stadium against Jock Hobbs' team. The All Blacks – who had already defeated both England (twice) and Australia earlier in the year – went into the first of the two tests expecting to cruise, despite having three debutants in their midst. First five-eighth Grant Fox, centre Victor Simpson and prop Steve McDowell were given their first test jerseys ahead of incumbents Wayne Smith, Steven Pokere and the injured Gary Knight.

As was the norm when teams played Argentina, scuffles broke out early in the match. "We are not dirty players," says Porta. "We are passionate. When we play in the Puma jersey, we are playing for all of Argentina. Also it's important when you play a team like New Zealand that you show them that you are prepared to battle with them. You can't be weak. You have to show them that you are strong. You have to show them that you will fight until the end."

It was obvious that this Argentine side was not going to lie down and concede defeat to the All Blacks. After an early Kieran Crowley penalty and a converted try from John Kirwan many would have expected a New Zealand rout. But the 9-0 deficit was cut to only two points soon afterwards when a Porta penalty was followed by a try from winger Juan Lanza. Before the halftime break Grant Fox would kick a drop goal and Crowley a penalty before Porta set up a try for centre Cuesta Silva, cutting the All Black lead to 15-14.

"At halftime we knew we had a chance to win," says Porta. "I think we had surprised them a little. But the All Blacks were a great team. We knew we would have to play to our very top level to make a victory a reality."

The Crowley/Porta kicking duel continued with both men slotting home two more penalties before the test was broken open by Victor Simpson. He intercepted a Puma pass and combined with John Kirwan and David Kirk to set Crowley up for the try. Two minutes later Kirwan had his second try before Jock Hobbs touched down at the end of the game. The All Blacks had won 33-20.

"It was disappointing," Porta says. "With the passing of time you look back at a test like that and you are proud that Argentina were so competitive against a team like New Zealand. But at the time it was a tough loss to suffer. When you play a test match against a team like New Zealand you convince yourself that you are good enough to win.

"Of course the All Blacks were better players. They were bigger and in some cases stronger. But the passion of playing for your country means you can forget about that. Instead you think of the people you are playing for. You think of the opportunity to make history and become the first side from Argentina to beat them. You believe you can win."

If nothing else the loss fuelled the Pumas' desire to put things right in the second test a week later. While Argentina went into the test unchanged, the All Blacks made three changes – Gary Whetton returned to the side to replace the injured Murray Pierce while the experienced inside-back combination of Dave Loveridge and Wayne Smith replaced David Kirk and Grant Fox.

As they had in the first test, the All Blacks took control early. Murray Mexted scored a pushover try but the score was soon locked up at 6-6 after Porta kicked the second of his four penalties. Before halftime, both All Black wingers – John Kirwan and Craig Green – had scored tries but Argentina were still in touch with Porta's third penalty meaning his side trailed only 18-9 at the break.

What happened next is still one of the most talked about chapters in the history of Argentine rugby. An early Porta dropped goal in the second half made the score 18-12. Midway through the half Porta turned the game on its head when he landed two more dropped goals in quick succession, levelling the scores at 18-18.

In the 66th minute Kieran Crowley kicked his solitary penalty before a Wayne Smith dropped goal attempt three minutes later narrowly missed its target. Then it was Porta's turn again. He slotted home his fourth penalty and the score was locked at 21-21. Kieran Crowley had a late opportunity to win the game for the All Blacks but his kick struck an upright and the Pumas held on to gain a memorable draw. Porta's personal tally of 21 points was the highest individual tally ever lodged against New Zealand.

"That day was a magic day," says Porta. "We played like All Blacks. I have spoken to many players about the joys of playing the All Blacks and they all say that if you are to have any success against them you must take every opportunity that comes your way. We had our chances to win the game but we were happy to settle for the draw. It meant so much to the people of Argentina.

"Of course, rugby will never compete with soccer for popularity in Argentina but for a day everyone was talking about the Pumas. Rugby was on everyone's lips. It didn't matter to me that I had scored all the points. People wanted to turn me into some kind of a hero. But it wasn't Hugo Porta's day. It was Argentina's day."

That the Pumas, for a day at least, were the equal of the All Blacks was remarkable. No other country has clung more fervently to amateurism. The foundations of the game in Argentina, as elsewhere in the world, are English. Expatriates established schools and encouraged students to play rugby instead of soccer.

Then there were tours from overseas, but especially there was the influence of South Africans – Barry Heatlie in the first decade of the century visited with the Junior Springboks and then Izak van Heerden prepared the Argentine national team for their first tour abroad in 1965.

An undoubted key to any Argentine rugby success has been their scrum. They developed a scrummaging technique beyond what has been achieved elsewhere in the world – the powerful *bajada* scrum. But the problem Argentine rugby faced is that to this day they have not developed their game away from the confines of the scrum.

Between 1971 and 1990 they could get away with it because Porta was there to bail them out of trouble. It's no coincidence that since Porta retired there have been few significant results posted by the Pumas.

"Rugby is a ball game and it must be played by 15 men," he says. "I don't like 10-man rugby. I enjoy watching a team like France. They look to attack at every opportunity. It's exciting to watch. It's entertainment.

"For many years we worked hard on our scrum. We had a good scrum but our game was very slow. We were not a very dynamic side. When we decided to run the ball – as we did against the All Blacks in 1985 – we had some success. For us it was a case of convincing ourselves that we could do it. Everything was based around the scrum and there's no doubt that sometimes we relied on it too much. I often wonder how good we could have been if we had developed our back play a little more. We had a lot of talented backs who had to spend many minutes watching the forwards."

While Porta was there, there was little reason to worry about Argentina's future. It would be out-of-touch to describe Porta as only a goalkicker. He had tremendous skill and pace and had switched to first-five on the suggestion of Pumas coach and mentor Angel Guastella in the early 1970s. Once installed at No 10 he became one of the best playmakers the world has ever seen. He could weave in and out of the tightest defences and tormented opposition flankers for nearly two decades. Yet he believes that, despite critics blaming today's laws for ruining the creativity of first-fives, his successors have never had it so good.

"I think that first-fives now undoubtedly have more time to make decisions than in my time. The flankers have to stay bound to the scrum – they are not allowed to move. As a result you have quite a lot of time to make decisions. It's nothing to do with the pace of the game. It's faster than when I used to play but being a first-five it seems you have more time to think about what you want to do."

Porta's third and only other test appearance against the All Blacks came during the 1987 World Cup. Argentina were drawn in the same pool as New Zealand, Italy and Fiji and were expected to at least be competitive. But the game was a low point for Porta. He was so disillusioned with his side's effort in the 46-15 mauling that he temporarily retired from international rugby after the tournament.

"It was a frustrating day," says Porta. "We had gone to New Zealand with high hopes but our dreams were shattered. Yes, the New Zealand team were a great team, but we didn't play the way we should have."

While Porta kicked three penalties and converted Juan Lanza's second-half try, it was too little too late. The All Blacks were in an attacking mood. After registering 70 points against both Italy and Fiji, it was obvious they wouldn't be content with just a victory against Argentina. The New Zealand forwards – with newcomers like Zinzan Brooke and Alan Whetton in sensational form – completely dominated the celebrated Puma pack, paving the way for a try-fest which saw David Kirk, Zinzan Brooke, Joe Stanley, Andy Earl, Kieran Crowley and Alan Whetton all score tries.

It was a frustrating day for Porta. The levels that he set for himself, and almost always reached, were beyond some of his teammates. The master craftsman was on a different level from the other Puma players. While the modest Porta would never agree with a statement like that, it was a fact. It was something that he had to make adjustments for.

"I would never criticise my teammates for not being good enough," he says. "If a player is selected to play for Argentina, then he is good enough to play for Argentina. Of course, every player who wears the Puma jersey has my respect. Sometimes there will be players who maybe aren't as good as some of the other players in the team. That kind of thing would happen more often in the Argentina side than in the All Black side because New Zealand has so much depth. But if such a player exists, then it is up to me to try and help him. You can only ask your players to give every game one hundred percent. If they are not as good as their opponents, then so be it. I would not get upset with my players if I knew that they had tried their hardest. Most of the time, the Puma players were true to their jersey. The pride they felt to play for Argentina almost always meant that they would perform to the best of their ability.

"Against New Zealand in the World Cup we lost a little bit of our discipline because of the frustration of playing such a fine side. But even if we had played to our best potential, I don't think the All Blacks were beatable. It was the best All Black side that I saw. They had a perfect balance between experienced players like Gary Whetton, Murray Pierce and John Kirwan and young stars like Michael Jones, Zinzan Brooke and Grant Fox."

⋅⋅⋅

WHAT is that saying? Something about how you can take the man out of rugby but you can't take the rugby out of the man... It's a statement that could have been written exclusively for Hugo Porta.

Since retiring from rugby Porta has become the Minister of Sport in Argentina. From his office he can see the stadium where he starred for the Pumas. And in a soccer-dominated country he is determined to see rugby grow.

"Rugby does not need to compete with soccer," he says. "Soccer is too big, too popular. We have to work hard trying to make the game more popular by giving players more opportunities to practise the game by giving them more facilities. My dream is to have every boy in Argentina with the chance to play rugby. Of course many will still play soccer, but if they have a chance to play our great game, they might take it. Instead of being the next Maradona, they could be the next Hugo Porta."

Unlike most politicians, Porta doesn't sugar-coat his words when it comes to the issue of overseas coaches taking charge of the Pumas. Former All Black coach Alex Wyllie was in charge of the Argentina side at last year's World Cup... something that Porta is still upset about.

"New Zealand has a lot to offer the world," he says. "There are many players and coaches from New Zealand with contracts around the world spreading the rugby gospel. I have no problem with that but I don't agree with a New Zealander coaching the Pumas. It's a wrong move. Not because it's Alex Wyllie, but because we are Latins. We feel differently from what a New Zealander does. We are closer to the French way of thinking than to the New Zealand way."

When Porta talks about rugby he talks with a glint in his eye and a passion in his voice... but there is no hiding his fear for the future of the game in Argentina.

"Rugby is in crisis here," he says. "The game is growing but the arrival of professionalism could tear the game apart. We have

HUGO PORTA'S TEST RECORDS

Argentine statistics vary greatly. These are the official statistics for tests for which the Argentine Rugby Union awarded Hugo Porta caps. The opposition were the South African Gazelles, Romania, Ireland, Scotland, France, Wales, New Zealand, England, Italy, Australia, South Africa, Fiji, Canada, Spain, Italy and the World XV.

There are also other matches that the Argentine Rugby Union would not regard as tests – against Chile, Brazil, Paraguay and Uruguay. In those 10 matches Porta scored 126 points.

His points record in international rugby is as follows:

Official tests: 57 games, 5 tries, 55 conversions, 109 penalties, 25 drop goals, 532 points

Unofficial tests: 9 games, 7 tries, 36 conversions, 6 penalties, 3 drop goals, 124 points

already lost a number of players to overseas teams – 'Topo' Rodriguez and Patricio Noriega to Australia and Diego Dominguez to Italy – and now of course there are many clubs around the world looking to sign up our players as well. I fear that it won't be long before 90 percent of the players in Argentina will be amateur and the rest will be an elite 10 percent that will be professional. The danger is that in time the two groups will grow further and further apart meaning we will have even less depth than we have now.

"That's the crisis. It is already coming increasingly difficult to close the gap on New Zealand, Australia and South Africa because rugby has developed there in such a way that there is a lot of money around to keep the elite players playing in their countries."

Porta is convinced the only way to stop the rot is for Argentina to be granted a place in an expanded Super 12 competition.

"I hear New Zealand talking about wanting the game to be

global," he says. "Well, it is not going to be a strong global game without South America playing a big part. Maybe the Tri-Nations countries think they can build the game globally without us but it can only be hurting rugby as a whole if they continue to ignore us. Surely the more depth you have at the top of the game the better it is for the sport.

"In the past when teams played Argentina they knew it was going to be a very tough, physical confrontation. That is still the case but there have been more and more lapses recently. Unless we are assisted in getting more regular tough competition, the harder it will be for us to keep in touch with the southern hemisphere giants. If we are allowed to stagnate, rugby as a whole will suffer."

Porta makes no apologies for his straight talking. He played his rugby with a raw determination and he has carried that attitude through to his politics.

"The simple fact is this," he says. "The quality of Argentina's rugby future lies in the hands of our old rivals Australia, South Africa and New Zealand. Rugby in Argentina has a proud history so there is no reason why we can't have a proud future. I just hope some of their administrators are listening."

HUGO PORTA AGAINST THE ALL BLACKS

Date	For	Venue	Result	Score	Points
30-10-76	Argentina	Buenos Aires	lost	9-21	dg
6-11-76	Argentina	Buenons Aires	lost	6-26	pen
8-9-79	Argentina	Dunedin	lost	9-18	pen, 2 dg
15-9-79	Argentina	Wellington	lost	6-15	2 pens
26-10-85	Argentina	Buenos Aires	lost	20-33	3 pens, dg
2-11-85	Argentina	Buenos Aires	drew	21-21	4 pen, 3 dg
1-6-87	Argentina	Wellington	lost	15-46	con, 3 pens

TEST MATCH CAREER

	P	W	L	D	T	C	P	Dg	Pts
vs All Blacks	7	-	6	1	-	1	14	7	65
All Tests	66	28	33	5	12	91	115	28	656

Gary Teichmann

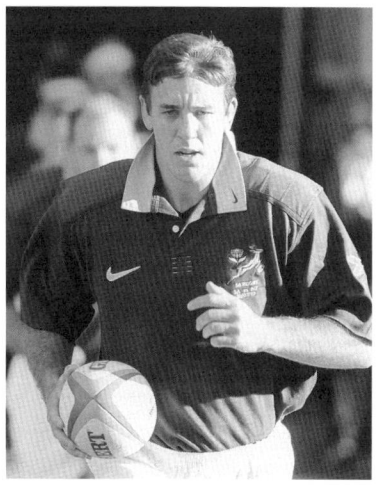

Date of birth: 9-1-1967
Born at: Gwelo, Zimbabwe
Position: No 8
Test matches: 42

"Gary Teichmann was the consummate Springbok forward – tough and uncompromising. It didn't matter what was going on around him because you always knew he would be one of the toughest competitors on the field. He had a never-say-die attitude that was worth admiring"

Zinzan Brooke

ISN'T it ironic? When Gary Teichmann was unexpectedly handed the Springbok captaincy it came during a series with the All Blacks. Teichmann's career high was chalked up against New Zealand – the same country which a year earlier had seen him sink to the lowest of lows. And just when Teichmann thought he knew what it was like to be standing in the deepest valley, the All Blacks provided a knock-out punch that would put an end to his international career. Isn't it ironic?

"The irony is not lost on me," he says. "In many ways the All Blacks have been the yardstick I have been judged on throughout my career. When you are good enough to beat them you know things are going well. When you fail against them it's as though the world turns on you. There's no middle ground in the rivalry between South Africa and New Zealand. You're either standing on the mountain top or you're crawling around at the bottom of the hill wondering what went wrong."

When Teichmann arrived in Dunedin in 1999 for the first Tri-Nations test of the year he couldn't have known that the last chapter in his captaincy was about to be played out. He went into the game with dreams of captaining the Springboks in the World Cup. He ended the game on the wrong side of a 28-0 scoreline and within days had learned that he would never play for South Africa again.

"If we'd beaten the All Blacks, who is to say that I wouldn't have gone on to play in the World Cup," says Teichmann. "It's not something I try to think about because the wound is still fresh. But it wasn't to be. The All Black team we faced in Dunedin was a very focused one. They were determined to get back on track after the disappointments of 1998 and we were put in our place. Perhaps if it hadn't been such a rampant All Black side I may have survived in the job for a little longer."

There are many similarities between All Black and Springbok rugby. The passion of both sets of players is well documented. The preoccupation of both sets of fans with their national teams is just as intense. The two countries are also linked by the common belief that losing is unacceptable.

The list of All Blacks who have been dropped after an All Black loss is a long one. The South Africans have a similar way of dealing with defeat, as Teichmann was to find out after the Dunedin drubbing. Springbok coach Nick Mallett "encouraged" his captain to step down for the game against Australia seven days later after Teichmann had picked up a slight knee strain. Initial reports from the South African management suggested Teichmann's injury would keep him out for six weeks but that was merely a smokescreen to buy Mallett time before he delivered the news to the heartbroken captain.

The New Zealand defeat was the last straw for Mallett, who two weeks earlier had to sit through a 29-19 loss to Wales at the Millennium Stadium. It didn't matter to him that Teichmann had been at the helm during the side's record-equalling 17-test-winning run which had ended only eight months – and three tests – earlier. Privately, Mallett described Teichmann as being "punch drunk". It was time to add his name to the Springbok scrap heap.

"It was a surprise when the news broke that I had been dropped," says Teichmann. "But looking back now, there were some pretty clear signs that the writing was on the wall for me. By the time we arrived in New Zealand I am convinced that Nick had already made up his mind about me. I just don't think he had the confidence to actually make the decision.

"While we were in Wales the communication between us stopped. He was no longer seeking me out for advice. We used to talk a lot. I think there was a time when he valued my opinion. There was even less communication in New Zealand. We would go through training sessions almost without a word being spoken between us. At the time I just put it down to the pressure that we were all under. I sensed something was wrong but I never thought it was as serious as it turned out to be. But it's obvious now he wanted me out. I don't think I could have done anything against the All Blacks that would have changed his mind."

Teichmann was hardly a weak link in the loss. The All Blacks, fresh from wins against Manu Samoa and France, were desperate for a win against their old rivals after losing five tests in a row (two to South Africa and three to Australia) in 1998. And while John Hart's All Blacks deserved to win the test, the 28-0 scoreline flattered them. The injury-hit South African pack gained parity against their All Black counterparts and the Boks had a try disallowed just after halftime, when the score was 6-0, when Teichmann was adjudged to have knocked on. Television replays later showed that Australian referee Peter Marshall had erred.

But the fact that South Africa had been held scoreless by New Zealand for the first time in 34 years couldn't be ignored. While the inexperienced Springbok inside backs Dave van Hoesslin and Gaffie du Toit struggled to direct play with any level of efficiency, All Black halfback Justin Marshall and first five-eighth Andrew Mehrtens were in dominating mood. This allowed their outsides to shine, with Marshall, Christian Cullen and Jeff Wilson all scoring tries in condemning the Springboks to a record loss.

"I was the scapegoat," says Teichmann. "The hard part about it was that I didn't think I was playing particularly poorly. If I felt like I had had two shocking games then it would have been easier to accept. I didn't think I was below par against the All Blacks. I'd had a poor first half against Wales but by the end of the game I thought I was making a worthwhile contribution to the side. But Nick was obviously of another opinion. The coach has the right to make decisions like the one Nick made. It probably didn't help that the All Blacks had played so well. I think the fact that we failed to score against them probably made it a little easier for Nick to look for someone to blame."

Mallett, who took charge of the Springboks at the beginning of the 1998 season, was determined to shape his side on the model of the All Blacks of 1996 and 1997. He was a great admirer of New Zealand's ability to produce teams that ran the ball at every opportunity. It was a style introduced by Laurie Mains in 1994 and carried on by John Hart into the 1996 and 1997 seasons. But Mallett's desire to play a similar style of rugby was his downfall in the early part of the 1999 season.

Says Teichmann: "I don't know why Nick was intent on changing the style of game that we played. It didn't make sense. We had a lot of success playing a forward-dominated game. But all of a sudden he wanted us to run around like headless chickens. It's all very well saying you want to play the way the All Blacks had played in the past but we didn't have the players for that style of rugby. There is no point asking a guy like Gaffie du Toit to play like Andrew Mehrtens. Gaffie is a good player but he's not Andrew Mehrtens. There's only one Andrew Mehrtens and he doesn't wear the Springbok jersey."

Teichmann's sacking sent shockwaves through world rugby. He was highly respected by his opponents and one of the people who took the time to console him was the All Black captain who confronted him in six tests in the 1996 and 1997 seasons. "I talked to Sean Fitzpatrick and he told me that when he retired from international rugby he felt like a massive weight had been lifted off his shoulders. He was consumed by a feeling of relief. I haven't reached that stage yet... maybe in time I will.

"At the moment I just feel like I was cheated out of playing in the World Cup. Nick Mallett thought I wasn't good enough. I think he was wrong, but his word means more than mine when it comes to selecting the Springboks."

❧

GARY TEICHMANN'S reputation was in free fall. Regarded not so long ago as the consummate Springbok captain, he had now been driven to the edge of despair. The All Blacks had once again savaged his Springboks. There was no avoiding the fact that as the captain he was first in the firing line. He could handle the pressure from within. The second-guessing of the coaching staff, the minor rumblings within the squad... that was the easy part. What drove Teichmann to the brink of handing in his Springbok jersey was worse than any defeat the All Blacks had handed out, and much more personal.

"No player should have to go through what I went through," he says. "It still hurts talking about it now."

Teichmann is talking about a stream of threatening hate mail he received in 1997 after the Springboks returned from their Tri-Nations battles against the All Blacks and Wallabies – vicious letters holding him personally responsible for the beatings South Africa had received against Australia at Ballymore (32-20) and New Zealand at Eden Park (55-33).

"At the time it was quite devastating. I was ready to walk away from international rugby. I couldn't understand how people could turn on me like that. I had always given everything I possibly could to the Springbok jersey. I was extremely proud to wear it and I would never not give one hundred percent. But despite that, some people really hated me. For a while it was too much and I'd convinced myself that I'd played my last game for the Springboks."

Helping make the decision to remain in the job was a lesson Teichmann had learned when he first made the Springbok team in 1996. Overlooked for the 1995 World Cup, he had been pulled into a team that was in many ways still suffering from a World Cup hangover. The South Africans played their first Tri-Nations game against the All Blacks in Christchurch without winger Chester Williams, centre Hennie le Roux, first five-eighth Joel

Stransky, halfback Joost van der Westhuizen, locks Kobus Weise and Hannes Strydom, hooker Chris Rossouw and prop Balie de Swart – all of whom had starred in the World Cup final triumph against New Zealand.

The world champions outscored the All Blacks one try to none but lost the test 15-11 – all of New Zealand's points coming from penalty kicks by Andrew Mehrtens. The South African media called for blood.

"It was a ridiculous reaction," says Teichmann. "Our press either didn't look into the circumstances or understand the circumstances. We were playing without a host of guys who had been in the team the year before and we had a new coach. I don't want to make excuses for losing that test but how can any reasonable person expect a team to just pick up from where they left off with all of that going on? It was very apparent to me that the media, as they do in New Zealand, just want results. It was an early lesson. It didn't matter under what conditions or circumstances you played, you just had to win."

Another lesson his first game against New Zealand produced was to never underestimate the intensity of an All Black/Springbok encounter.

Teichmann, who spent his formative years in Zimbabwe, had never dreamed of playing for the Springboks. He wasn't a student of the game. His knowledge of the rivalry was limited. He knew the All Blacks were the enemy, but he didn't always know why. But within the first few minutes of his first encounter with New Zealand he'd learn everything he needed to know.

"Things blew up as soon as the first scrum went down," he says. "The front rows were having a go at each other. It was nerve wracking. I knew then that this wasn't Mickey Mouse stuff. This was test match rugby the way it should be played. The line had been drawn in the ground. I knew that there was no way I could take a backwards step to these guys."

Leading the All Black charge was Sean Fitzpatrick. Hated by the South African public who perceived him as a cheat – they labelled him as a "dirty" player – the New Zealand captain drew nothing but admiration from the Springbok players.

"When you grow up you hear stories about the great players –

whether they be Springboks or All Blacks," says Teichmann. "I am sure that in a few years, if they are not already, children in both countries will be hearing about Sean Fitzpatrick. It's true that he is disliked by many South Africans but in a way that is born out of respect. The guy was a warrior. You don't play that amount of games as a hooker and captain of New Zealand if you're not tough.

"The All Blacks had a lot of great players playing for them in 1996. You had guys like Zinzan Brooke, Frank Bunce, Craig Dowd and Olo Brown... but the team revolved around Fitzpatrick. He really was the heart and soul of that team. I was lucky enough to play under François Pienaar, who was a great leader of men. Fitzpatrick seemed to have the same qualities. He was the sort of player you'd rather have in your team than in the opposition."

Fitzpatrick and his All Blacks were determined to set the record straight in 1996 after the disappointments of the World Cup. After the Christchurch test the New Zealanders headed to South Africa for a Tri-Nations match, which would be followed by a three-test series.

"We knew we were going to be involved in a very hard battle," says Teichmann. "In many ways the All Blacks were the best side at the World Cup but a tremendous spirit and a lot of fantastic defence ensured that the Springboks ended the year as world champions. I can't imagine what that would have been like for the All Blacks to swallow. I don't think you can even begin to understand what those New Zealanders went through unless you were standing in their shoes. But one thing is for sure, when they showed up it was obvious their singular goal was to prove to the world that they were capable of beating the Springboks in South Africa. They were on a mission."

When the teams headed into the Tri-Nations test at Newlands, confidence within the Springbok camp was high. Their World Cup hero Joel Stransky was back in the side along with 1995 hooker John Allan. Stransky needed only four minutes to land the first penalty of the match. Then, after Andrew Mehrtens had replied for the All Blacks, the Springboks went on the rampage. Within the first 26 minutes of the test they had scored two tries. Second five-eighth Jaapie Mulder and prop Os du Randt's tries had helped the Boks to a 15-6 halftime lead.

"Anytime you have a lead like that in a test match you have to back yourself to hang on to it," says Teichmann. "And we certainly did. We didn't relax or think the game was won. We knew the All Black reply wouldn't be far away... we just had to make sure that we were ready for it."

After the lead had been extended to 18-6 by Stransky's boot, the turning point came. Pienaar was carried from the field after picking up a neck injury. South Africa's answer to Sean Fitzpatrick was carried from the field on a stretcher. The Boks wouldn't score again. In contrast, Glen Osborne and Craig Dowd would touch down for the All Blacks and with Mehrtens kicking a further three penalty goals and two conversions New Zealand registered a comfortable 29-18 victory.

Teichmann didn't have time for despondency over the loss. Once it became apparent that Pienaar's test career was over, he was summoned by coach Andre Markgraaf, who handed him the captaincy. If playing the All Blacks was a daunting proposition, leading a disjointed Springbok team in a home test series against them was unnerving for the new captain.

"We weren't in the best possible shape going into the series... there was no denying that," Teichmann says. "We'd just lost our captain and there I was, playing in my sixth test, taking over. I was shocked to be offered the job.

"I never doubted my ability to lead the team. I'd been the Natal captain in 1995 and was confident that I could read a game well and make the necessary adjustments on the field. But I had no idea what the outside pressures were going to be like. I was thrust into the limelight. The press were building me up and I'd been around long enough to know that if things didn't go well I'd be the one who would have to have the answers for them.

"Looking back, I can't say too much good about our media. Obviously, you would prefer to have them willing you on to win rather than accepting a defeat but sometimes it gets out of hand. The press put far too much pressure on the players. When things go wrong you need people to help you climb out of the mess... you don't need people taking shots at you because all that does is make the pressure on the players mount."

Teichmann didn't have to wait long for the pressure on him to build. The first of the three tests at Durban was set alight in the fourth minute when All Black winger Jeff Wilson scored a try. Before halftime fullback Christian Cullen had added his name to the score sheet, assisting the New Zealanders to a 15-9 lead at the break. Zinzan Brooke effectively sealed the test for the All Blacks with a 48th-minute try, although a late try from Springbok centre Danie van Schalkwyk ensured the 23-19 scoreline was respectable.

The loss was accepted with disdain in South Africa. The Boks were a test away from losing their first series against New Zealand in the republic.

"The pressure was immense," says Teichmann. "One year we were the world champions and the next we were on the verge of the unacceptable. We still believed in ourselves but it was obvious that we'd have to play the test of our lives to beat that All Black side. They were a great team – the best that I had played against. If you had a chink in your armour they would find it. They were masters at finding your weakness.

"So often when you play New Zealand you find yourself saying *we could have* or *we should have* but it was often the case that *we didn't*. You only get your just rewards against them if you play your absolute best. We were unable to reach those standards."

If Fitzpatrick's team were playing for every All Black who had ever returned to New Zealand after a series loss in South Africa, the Springboks were playing with the weight of a nation of their shoulders. For them, rugby's greatest rivalry didn't need a chapter which headlined All Black success away from the comfort zones of Dunedin, Christchurch, Wellington and Auckland. But the chapter was written emphatically when the All Blacks won the second test in Pretoria 33-26. One of the All Black stars that day was Zinzan Brooke, who sealed the victory with a 78th-minute dropped goal.

"As a neutral fan watching on the television it would have been marvellous viewing," says Teichmann. "As a No 8 you always want to test yourself against the best No 8s in the world but with Zinny I don't think comparisons were fair. The guy was a freak! What other No 8 makes a habit of dropping goals? Zinzan was a big strong man with the skills of a couple of backs. I don't think too many No 8s around the place can claim that kind of make-up."

With the series lost and the South African rugby fraternity in a state of mourning, Markgraaf and Teichmann set about trying to lift their troops for the third test in Johannesburg a week later. The pressure could not have been greater. With the Tri-Nations matches taken into account, the All Blacks had beaten the Springboks in four consecutive tests. It was an embarrassing statistic which threatened to hang around the necks of the Boks for the rest of their careers.

"When the pressure comes, you have a choice," says Teichmann. "You can run and hide or you can live with it. I don't care how strong you may think you are, the pressure will always get to you. If the press is having a go at you or the people in the street are screaming abuse, it gets to you. The key is to not carry that pressure on the field with you. As soon as it starts affecting your game then you are in trouble. My whole attitude at the time was to concentrate on rebuilding the team. We had to get a good performance from each player if we were going to have a chance to stop the bleeding."

All Black coach John Hart understandably had trouble motivating his players – physically exhausted and mentally wasted – for the Ellis Park test. Nevertheless, even with the series effectively "dead", the pressure on the Boks remained... and this time they responded. Both teams would score three tries – Joost van der Westhuizen, with two, and Andre Joubert touching down for the Springboks and Sean Fitzpatrick, Walter Little and Justin Marshall scoring for New Zealand – but it was the boots of Joubert and Henry Honiball that would be the difference as South Africa registered a 32-22 win.

"It didn't matter to us that the win came after the All Blacks had won the series," says Teichmann. "It may have been difficult for some of them to get up for the test but that's no excuse. Every time you pull on your country's jersey there can be no excuses. I'm sure that the passion the New Zealand players have for the All Black jersey is just as strong as the feeling we have for the South African one. That's why that win is still a very significant one for all the guys who played that day. The All Blacks have never laid down in a test match and given up. I can assure you that any win you get against the All Blacks is significant. After what they'd put us through in the four previous tests, there was a real feeling of pride in the way that we had turned things around."

The Ellis Park win ensured the Springboks left for their summer tour in a positive frame of mind. And their confidence grew with test wins against Argentina (twice), France (twice) and Wales. They seemed to be over the problems that plagued them during the Tri-Nations and subsequent All Black tour. But as the players were beginning to think that Tri-Nations success in 1997 might be possible, a bombshell hit South African rugby. A secretly taped telephone conversation with coach Andre Markgraaf was aired on the South African Broadcasting Corporation's evening news which had Markgraaf using the word "kaffir" – an offensive pejorative used by right-wing whites against blacks – in reference to senior black rugby officials. *It's kaffirs. It's the fucking NSC, the fucking kaffirs.*

Markgraaf resigned immediately and within days was replaced by Carel du Plessis. The transition wasn't a smooth one. The Boks followed their series loss at home to the All Blacks with a series loss to the British Lions. Then it was time to face up to Australia and New Zealand in the Tri-Nations. Within seven months of his appointment, du Plessis would be fired and replaced with Nick Mallett. Captaining the Springboks wasn't getting any easier.

"I can't help but have a lot of admiration for the way the game is run in New Zealand," says Teichmann. "I know things aren't perfect there but I can't see the day when the All Blacks have three different coaches in the space of 12 months.

"It was terribly disruptive. It's not easy to build a team with a common goal when the coach keeps changing. Each of them had his own ideas on how the game should be played and of course each of them had differing opinions on who should be wearing the Springbok jersey.

"South Africa will always struggle to match the consistency of a team like New Zealand because of the internal politics which exist in South African rugby. There's no question that New Zealand is miles ahead of us when it comes to the administration of the game. Believe me, South Africa is not the easiest place in the world to play rugby."

Du Plessis' stint in charge of the Springboks was doomed from the start. He was given the job despite having limited coaching experience and found it difficult to sell his ideas to a Springbok team that was quickly becoming disillusioned. The highs of the World Cup triumph were now replaced with bitter infighting. World Cup-winning coach Kitch Christie called for his captain François Pienaar to be reinstated after "a lack of leadership" from Teichmann in the Lions' series. And another former Bok coach, Natal's Ian McIntosh, had publicly declared his interest to return to the top job in Springbok rugby.

It was against that backdrop that Teichmann led his side into the first Tri-Nations battle of the year. Dissimilarly, John Hart's All Blacks fronted at Ellis Park with a settled side both on and off the field. The forward pack was unchanged from 1996 with the exception of the addition of Taine Randell in place of the ageing Michael Jones. The backs were arguably stronger than the previous season with Carlos Spencer in the No 10 jersey igniting a backline that was overdosing with the talents of Jeff Wilson, Tana Umaga and Christian Cullen.

Indeed, the All Blacks were in the midst of a purple patch. Since the World Cup Hart had prepared them for 14 tests and 13 of them had been won with Manu Samoa, Scotland, Fiji, Argentina, Australia and the Springboks on the receiving end. The solitary loss was the test at Ellis Park the previous year. That defeat alone was enough to ensure that the All Blacks were primed for the return game. There was another score to settle. Another battle to be won.

"Our confidence had taken a bit of a battering," says Teichmann. "The series loss against the Lions meant that the pressure was building on us again. Any confidence that we'd gained in Europe at the end of 1996 had been chipped away. I know that I still thought we'd beat the All Blacks but I'm not sure if that belief was as deep within some of the other guys. In the end that was probably what stopped us from hanging on for the win."

The Springboks started the game well and with Naka Drotske's sixth-minute try held a 10-0 advantage. After All Black centre Frank Bunce had pulled back a try, the Boks went further ahead when fullback Russell Bennett scored, helping them to a 23-7 lead. But any thoughts the Boks had of securing a famous victory where dashed by an All Black comeback that saw Bunce (again), Jeff Wilson and Carlos Spencer all score tries before a 69th-minute penalty from Spencer confirmed New Zealand's 35-32 win.

"It was a shattering defeat," says Teichmann. "It was another reminder of how ruthless the All Blacks are. They simply refused to accept defeat. Just when you think you've got them right where you want them, one of their players will do something inspirational and the rest follow. It was a remarkable effort from them because many teams would have crumbled with the sort of pressure we'd put them under earlier in the game. But not the All Blacks. We'd put up a brave fight but they really were on a different level from us."

By the time the Boks arrived in Auckland for the return test at Eden Park, they were in disarray. They'd lost to Australia 32-20 in Brisbane the week before and the lack of understanding from the players for du Plessis' ideas meant that the relationship between the side's management and players was at breaking point. Something had to give and in the end it was the players' resolve that gave way.

The All Blacks cantered to a then-record 55-35 win, scoring a remarkable seven tries against a Springbok defence that wasn't helped by the sending off of Andre Venter early in the second half. The gap between the two sides was obvious to see. One side, high on confidence, played a champagne style of rugby while the other lacked cohesion. It was the low point of Teichmann's reign.

"We got an absolute hiding," he says. "We'd had a disruptive build-up to the test. There was a lot of talk about Carel being replaced and players being dropped and it didn't help that the understanding between the players and the coach wasn't one hundred percent there. But there's no point making excuses. When you play test rugby you can't expect everything to be rosy. The test of a great team comes when you have to face adversity. It's easy to win games when everything is close to perfect off the field. It's when you have had to take a few hits and have to fight on that greatness comes. We certainly took a few hits at Eden Park but we didn't respond. It was terribly disappointing. There certainly didn't seem to be any light at the end of the tunnel."

ɕ⹁

IT seemed like the perfect partnership. Both were men of strict morals and high principles. One was the visionary and the other the faithful disciple. They would reach incredible highs in the 22 months they worked together. They came together as virtual strangers. They grew alongside each other and became friends. They parted as bitter rivals.

"It's not easy for me to say bad things about Nick Mallett," says Gary Teichmann. "I was disappointed with the way things turned out. I didn't think he treated me with the respect I deserved at the end of our rugby relationship. Instead of confronting me and being honest with me, he just ignored me. But Nick Mallett did a tremendous amount of good for me as well. I had great respect for him. He took over the Springboks when we were in desperate need of rescuing and he rebuilt us into the world force that we had been in the past.

"A lot of the credit has to go to the players for that turnaround but the fact is, Nick Mallett was at the helm. He deserves just as much, if not more, credit. I doubt if we would have had the sort of success we had through the latter part of 1997 and 1998 without him."

The decision to replace Carel du Plessis with Mallett was a master stroke. The first thing he did when appointed to the job was to fly to Durban to meet senior Natal Springboks like Teichmann, Adrian Garvey, Mark Andrews, Steve Atherton, Andre Joubert and Henry Honiball. He believed in empowering his players. He sought out their opinions and, unlike some of the men who'd preceded him, valued them.

"I felt pretty comfortable with the way he approached the game," says Teichmann. "The great thing about Nick was that, in those days anyway, he told it like it was. There were never any wishy-washy statements. Everyone knew exactly where they stood with him. It was obvious from the start that he was not the type of man that you wanted to cross. He was a hard taskmaster but the players like that. We wanted to be in a position where we could learn. We started to enjoy our rugby again."

Teichmann and his teammates responded to Mallett with a vigour that had been missing from the side since 1995. At the end of 1997 the Springboks headed to the northern hemisphere for a tour that would be a turning point for South African rugby. Wins against Italy, France, England and Scotland were recorded. Before the Tri-Nations the following year there were more test victories.

Ireland were beaten 37-3 and 33-0 in their two tests in the republic before Wales were slaughtered 96-13 and England dispatched by a 18-0 scoreline.

Ten tests in succession had been won but Teichmann knew the real challenge was just around the corner. The Tri-Nations draw pitted them against Australia in Perth and New Zealand in Wellington.

"Everyone had been thrilled with the way we'd been going but the real gauge of our progress was going to come in those two tests," says Teichmann. "It was time to stand up and be counted. We knew it wouldn't be easy but our confidence was high. A year earlier I think some of us had been a little apprehensive about playing in Australia and New Zealand. But now we were back to the way every Springbok team should be. There was a real belief, a real determination. We wanted to show people that we were back to our best."

Australia, backing up from their 24-16 win against the All Blacks in Melbourne, couldn't capitalise on numerous chances against the Springboks and lost 14-13.

Ironically, it was the All Blacks' turn to be consumed with infighting. Since the last meeting between the teams at Eden Park the All Blacks had lost the services of the retired Sean Fitzpatrick, Zinzan Brooke and Frank Bunce. Taine Randell was the new captain of a team whose divisions were clear for all to see. There were massive splits in the squad with experienced players like Robin Brooke and Ian Jones shunning any leadership roles. Randell, in effect, was left to find his way on his own.

It was a recipe for disaster. While the All Blacks registered consecutive wins against the below-strength English tourists, the side's limitations were obvious during the loss in Melbourne. The new midfield combination of Walter Little and Scott McLeod was a failure and halfback Justin Marshall – rushed back after an Achilles injury – was off the pace.

"We knew they were there for the taking," says Teichmann. "But at the same time we also knew that we would still have to play our absolute best if we were going to beat them. When you play the All Blacks there is no room for error. All you have to do is look at the players they could still call on. Okay, they were missing three experienced guys but it wasn't as though it was a bad All Black side... I don't think there has ever been one of those."

Fittingly, the test between two of the game's greatest rivals was a throwback to the style of rugby that fans in the 1950s and 1960s had grown to appreciate. A solitary Percy Montgomery penalty was the only score of the first half. It then took 20 minutes of the second spell for Andrew Mehrtens to level the scores at 3-3 before another Springbok penalty and a 70th-minute try to winger Pieter Rossouw secured a 13-3 win – the first South African win on New Zealand soil since the second test of the 1981 series.

"There is nothing like beating the All Blacks," says Teichmann. "It is the greatest feeling in rugby. When you play rugby in South Africa and you first think about the possibility of pulling on the Springbok jersey, it is always the All Blacks you dream about playing against. You know that they will always provide the ultimate test.

"The win in Wellington was made even more special because of the hidings we had taken from them in the previous couple of years. In some of the tests we'd had a chance of beating them and failed; in others they had completely dominated us. But this time it was our turn. We'd made the breakthrough.

"It was an emotional day. I have never been in a changing room like it. The boys were just so thrilled to have beaten New Zealand. The Athletic Park changing rooms are notorious for being cold and miserable. On that day, the grey cement didn't seem to bother us... it felt like a palace!"

Three weeks later the teams met again, this time at Kings Park in Durban. The All Blacks reacted to the loss at Athletic Park and the subsequent 27-23 defeat at the hands of Australia in Christchurch by sacking test veterans Ian Jones, Michael Jones and Walter Little. Young Waikato lock Royce Willis was added to the starting XV along with Otago No 8 Isitolo Maka and Auckland centre Eroni Clarke.

"There was a new vibe within our squad by the time we assembled for the Durban test," says Teichmann. "Our confidence was on a high. We had reached a point where we felt like we couldn't be beaten. It would have been a dangerous state of mind if we'd been arrogant about it, but we weren't. We were just very confident.

Brian Moore prepares to feed a lineout during the 1995 World Cup semifinal at Cape Town. The All Blacks, led by four-try hero Jonah Lomu, demolished England 45-29.

Captain Courageous… François Pienaar brought great intensity to his role as Springbok captain.

François Pienaar leads the Springboks out to do battle with their most feared rivals, the All Blacks.

Argentinian captain Hugo Porta was always a hugely popular figure in New Zealand. Above he shows off his pois and, at right, his balance.

Richard Spranger, Photosport

Gary Teichmann takes a big hit during the high-scoring Tri Nations match between the Springboks and the All Blacks at Eden Park in 1997. New Zealand won the game 55-35.

JPR Williams gets his kick away despite the attentions of Ken Carrington during action from the 1971 series between the Lions and the All Blacks.

A bloodied JPR Williams leaves the field for treatment during the infamous All Blacks-Bridgend match in 1978.

When we looked at each other we knew we could rely on each other. We were a team... a very solid team."

That belief in themselves was the key. With 15 minutes left in the test the Springboks were 23-5 down. Maka had been inspirational and proved too powerful for the South African loose forward trio of Andre Venter, J Erasmus and Teichmann. But when Maka had to leave the field after being concussed the tide turned. Joost van der Westhuizen, Bobby Skinstad and James Dalton all scored tries – Dalton's controversial effort coming in injury time – to guide South Africa to a 24-23 win.

"I was thrilled with the way we came back," says Teichmann. "It's something the All Blacks are experts at doing. There have been plenty of tests down the years when the All Blacks look down and out only to come from nowhere to win. There is nothing more satisfying for a captain to see your team play their hearts out. The only way we were going to come back was by doing that. I asked the boys to lift and they did. It was one of the proudest days of my career. The fact that it came against the All Blacks made it even more special."

It was the All Blacks' fourth consecutive test defeat. Loss No 5 was only two weeks away – a 19-14 heartbreaker against Australia in Sydney. It was the second worst All Black season on record, something that provided Teichmann with no joy whatsoever.

"What genuine rugby people want is good competition," he says. "Nothing would make me happier than to see the Springboks beat the All Blacks – whether the All Blacks had an off day or not – every time the two countries played. But rugby needs the All Blacks to be strong. I know the rivalry between South Africa and New Zealand is a fierce one but that doesn't mean we want to see them lose to Australia and England all the time. I think that stems from the respect we have for the All Blacks... not just the traditions but the current players. You don't like to see people you admire suffering like that."

While the All Blacks spent the 1998 summer licking their wounds the Boks were on another northern hemisphere tour. Wins against Wales, Scotland and Ireland were recorded, stretching their winning streak to 17 games and equalling the record set by Wilson Whineray and Brian Lochore's All Black sides between 1965 and 1970. Many predicted Teichmann's men would break the record but

ALL BLACK WINNING STREAK (September '65 – July '70)	SPRINGBOK WINNING STREAK (November '97 – December '98)
1. 20-3 v South Africa (h)	1. 61-22 v Australia (h)
2. 20-3 v British Isles (h)	2. 62-31 v Italy (a)
3. 16-12 v British Isles (h)	3. 36-32 v France (a)
4. 19-6 v British Isles (h)	4. 52-10 v France (a)
5. 24-11 v British Isles (h)	5. 29-11 v England (a)
6. 29-9 v Australia (h)	6. 68-10 v Scotland (a)
7. 23-11 v England (a)	7. 37-13 v Ireland (h)
8. 13-6 v Wales (a)	8. 33-0 v Ireland (h)
9. 21-15 v France (a)	9. 96-13 v Wales (h)
10. 14-3 v Scotland (a)	10. 18-0 v England (h)
11. 27-11 v Australia (a)	11. 14-13 v Australia (a)
12. 19-18 v Australia (a)	12. 13-3 v New Zealand (a)
13. 12-9 v France (h)	13. 24-23 v New Zealand (h)
14. 9-3 v France (h)	14. 29-15 v Australia (h)
15. 19-12 v France (h)	15. 28-20 v Wales (a)
16. 19-0 v Wales (h)	16. 35-10 v Scotland (a)
17. 33-12 v Wales (h)	17. 27-13 v Ireland (a)

they fell at the final hurdle when they were defeated 13-7 by England at Twickenham.

South Africa was back in Europe six months later to play a one-off test against a rejuvenated Wales. It was a game the Springboks didn't want to play. The game fell only two weeks before the 1999 Tri-Nations opener against New Zealand in Dunedin and was lost by South Africa 29-19. As in 1996 and 1997, when the Boks were struggling to win, their press was quick to turn on them. It didn't seem to matter that they went into the test without their first-choice halfback Joost van der Westhuizen, first five-eighth Henry Honiball and flanker Bobby Skinstad.

The talented trio were still missing for the test against the All Blacks – a game that would turn out to be Teichmann's last in Springbok colours... the 28-0 scoreline condemning him to Mallett's axe.

"Imagine getting hold of the All Black side and taking Justin

Marshall, Andrew Mehrtens and Josh Kronfeld out of the team," says Teichmann. "In effect that's how we went into that test. We were missing three key guys and it was always going to be difficult to beat the All Blacks without them. But I can live with that. If I have walked off the field knowing that we have done our best and were beaten by the better team then that is acceptable to me. What I can't accept is the way the South African media tore into us.

"There were all sorts of rumours going around about tension within our squad between the Afrikaans and English-speaking players. But there has never been a problem between the players. If there was a misunderstanding it was between the management of the team and the union. The players had been through too much together to let things like our backgrounds get in the way of our rugby.

"I guess it's the curse of being a Springbok – once you earn the jersey you have to be prepared to live with the press watching every little thing you do. If nothing else, playing rugby in South Africa is… well, let's just say it's character building."

GARY TEICHMANN AGAINST THE ALL BLACKS

Date	For	Venue	Result	Score	Points
1-8-92	Natal	Durban	lost	25-43	
20-7-96	South Africa	Christchurch	lost	11-15	
10-8-96	South Africa	Cape Town	lost	18-29	
17-8-96	South Africa	Durban	lost	19-23	
24-8-96	South Africa	Pretoria	lost	26-33	
31-8-96	South Africa	Johannesburg	won	32-22	
19-7-97	South Africa	Johannesburg	lost	32-35	
9-8-97	South Africa	Auckland	lost	35-55	try
25-7-98	South Africa	Wellington	won	13-3	
15-8-98	South Africa	Durban	won	24-23	
10-7-99	South Africa	Dunedin	lost	0-28	

TEST MATCH CAREER

	P	W	L	D	T	C	P	Dg	Pts
vs All Blacks	10	3	7	-	1	-	-	-	5
All Tests	42	29	13	-	5	-	-	-	25

JPR Williams

Date of birth: 2-3-1949
Born at: Cardiff, Wales
Position: Fullback
Test matches: 63

"I always admired JPR Williams for his guts and his competitiveness and he was a dangerous counter-attacker. Among overseas fullbacks he set the main when the law encouraged fullbacks to initiate attacks"

Fergie McCormick
(**Fergie,** 1976)

IT is a day etched into Welsh rugby folklore… for all the wrong reasons. JPR Williams was three minutes away from captaining Wales to its first victory over the All Blacks for 25 years. Three minutes away from becoming Wales' most revered captain. Three minutes away from immortality.

It had been a remarkable game. This Welsh side of 1978 were without the stars who had made them the most dominant team in Europe. The likes of Gareth Edwards, Barry John and Phil Bennett had retired from international rugby but the new-look Welsh team were on the verge of history. With 77 minutes of the game already played, Wales led Graham Mourie's All Blacks 12-10. What followed was to become the most controversial moment in test history between these two teams since the infamous occasion at Cardiff Arms Park in 1905 when Bob Deans had a try disallowed in a 3-0 Welsh triumph.

Seventy-three years later, at the same ground, the All Blacks won a lineout 10 metres out from the Welsh 22. As the ball was thrown in, New Zealand lock Andy Haden dived out of the lineout. As he hit the Arms Park turf, English referee Roger Quittenton awarded a penalty to the All Blacks and Brian McKechnie slotted home the kick to give New Zealand a 13-12 win.

Immediately after the game Quittenton told reporters that he'd given the penalty for an infringement by the Swansea lock Geoff Wheel whom he detected had used the shoulder of All Black Frank Oliver for leverage when jumping. But the Welsh, to this day, are convinced Quittenton only used the incident involving Wheel as an afterthought when the realisation that he'd been hoodwinked by Haden dawned on him.

"It was sickening," says Williams. "Because I was playing fullback I hadn't seen the incident as it happened. I was too far away from the action. But I knew that something had gone terribly wrong by the reaction of the forwards after the game. It wasn't until the next day that I saw television replays of Andy diving out of the lineout. I burst into tears. We had been absolutely and totally cheated out of a famous victory. We would have been immortal if we'd won that game.

"I still find it hard to think about the feelings I had after watching the replays. To be fair to Andy, I'd seen other players dive out of lineouts to get a penalty before and I've seen it since. But I'm not sure if I condone that sort of behaviour. In fact, I know that I don't condone it. There is no room for cheating on the rugby field."

Williams had already gone a long way towards booking his place as an immortal in Welsh rugby years earlier when he toured New Zealand with the 1971 British Lions side.

Despite the side's coach Carwyn James – a former Welsh international – being able to field a backline that was second to none in world rugby at the time, few gave the Lions a chance of upsetting Colin Meads' All Blacks. The Lions backs boasted six Welsh players – halfback Edwards, first-five John, second-five John

Dawes, wingers Gerald Davies and John Bevan and Williams at fullback – but the old adage of "everything starts up front" looked like being James' Achilles heel. After all, when the Welsh toured in 1969, they toured with the superior backline but were hammered in the two-test series.

"I still have nightmares about that '69 series," says Williams. "I absolutely idolised the All Blacks and when I ran out onto Lancaster Park I can honestly say that it was one of the most daunting moments of my career. When the game started it seemed like there were a hundred All Blacks on the field. They were everywhere. The game was played at a pace that I hadn't experienced and before I knew it I found I was talking to myself, saying, 'Don't worry, forget about the occasion, just take the man with the ball.' It was an overpowering experience... very much a case of men against boys."

The first test was lost 19-0 while the second was marked by a world record haul of 24 points for All Black fullback Fergie McCormick as the New Zealanders cruised to a 33-12 win. While the All Blacks' series win wasn't unexpected – going into the series, the New Zealanders had won their previous 15 tests dating back to 1965 – the manner of the victories was devastating for the Welsh who had arrived in New Zealand as both Five Nations and Triple Crown champions.

"Even in the second test, when we managed to score a couple of tries, I don't think we ever felt as though we were on the same level as the All Blacks. If we'd been able to win a bit more ball I'm sure the backline we had could have caused a few problems but unfortunately our forwards threw in the towel on that tour. They were certainly no match for the All Black pack which was mightily led by Ian Kirkpatrick, Brian Lochore and Colin Meads."

All three New Zealand legends would feature in the Lions' tour two years later but the Welsh players in the British Isles team had taken aboard a number of lessons from their series whitewash and arrived back in New Zealand with many reasons to be confident.

"We all realised we hadn't been strong enough or fit enough to take on the All Blacks in '69 – either physically or mentally. For three months before the tour all the guys at London Welsh [Williams, Dawes and John Taylor] trained together every morning

– virtually as full-time professionals.

"It was hard work but we had to put ourselves through it because the thing that came back to Wales from the '69 tour was an admiration for the preparation of the All Blacks. I admired the attitude they seemed to have that the physical fitness side of things was the individual player's responsibility.

"In Wales the attitude that prevailed was that players would turn up to training at the end of summer and expect their coach to get them fit. That's rubbish. But it was the way things were then and in many respects it is still the attitude of a lot of club players. In New Zealand things were different. Their attitude was that if you weren't fit, the coach would tell you to piss off and come back in three months when you'd got yourself fit. It is a lovely attitude.

"The way I see it, if players haven't got the discipline to get themselves ready in the off-season, how are they ever going to have the discipline to devote themselves fully to the task of being an international footballer?"

With the knowledge that they had prepared better for the job ahead, the dominant Welsh contingent in the Lions' squad had a real belief in their ability to become the first British Isles squad to win a test series in New Zealand.

"There was still a big mental block to overcome," says Williams, "but knowing that we'd put the hard work in before getting to New Zealand certainly helped us. I know that, for me, it was the first time I felt like I could physically match myself with them. There was a massive task in front of us, a daunting task, but we were ready for battle. At the same stage of the '69 tour I don't think any of us really believed that."

Owing to a number of retirements, the New Zealand selectors were ruthless with their reaction to the lost series in South Africa in 1970 and for the first test of the new year, in Dunedin, they injected seven new players to the test ranks. With Malcolm Dick and Grahame Thorne out of the picture, star winger Bryan Williams was moved to centre, allowing the introduction of Bruce Hunter and Ken Carrington on the wings while Bob Burgess was given his debut at first-five. The new forwards were Ritchie Guy, Allan McNaughton, Peter Whiting and Tane Norton.

The new caps, especially the forwards, were impressive but despite New Zealand dominating possession the Lions won 9-3. The breakthrough had been made. The Lions' inside backs made good use of their limited ball with John in particular tormenting McCormick, so much so that the Canterbury fullback's international career was deemed over at the test's end.

"We were on the ropes for quite a while but even though New Zealand dominated the game, we had the confidence to hang in there," says Williams. "We were delighted when the final whistle went and we were 1-0 up in the series but it wasn't long before we started to think about the task ahead of us. The All Blacks were hugely disappointed after the game and we knew they'd come back stronger than ever in the second test. It was a sobering thought."

Williams' thoughts were prophetic. Laurie Mains and Alex Wyllie were brought into the New Zealand side for McCormick and Alan Sutherland respectively and thanks to an improved forward effort and more fluent backline (Williams had been restored to the wing in place of Carrington) the All Blacks levelled the series with a 22-12 result.

"One of the great joys about looking back at the tour was how we responded to that loss," says Williams. "I have no doubt a lot of British sides that have toured New Zealand – both before '71 and since – have suffered from a form of stage fright. Unless you have played against the All Blacks it is impossible to understand this great myth that goes with them. The history the All Blacks enjoy, the fanatical support they receive and the great amount of talent and power they possess have scared many teams into submission.

"And those black jerseys... I'm sure it makes them look bigger than they actually are. I remember having a few drinks with the New Zealand boys after a test and thinking 'they aren't any bigger than us!' On the field they look like bloody giants."

If the Lions had any thoughts of panicking after the All Blacks' victory in Christchurch, they had nothing on the New Zealand selectors of the day who replaced an injured Whiting with the semi-retired Lochore. The former All Black captain had played all of his previous tests 24 tests at No 8 but was asked to share the locking duties with Meads at Athletic Park. It was a move that failed miserably. The Lions dominated the lineouts, giving Edwards and John the best service of the tour as they made the lives of their New Zealand counterparts, Going and Burgess, miserable.

"One question I get asked is whether I knew fellows like Barry John and Gareth Edwards were great players at the time I was playing with them. The answer is absolutely yes. Both of them had the great ability to make everyone around them relaxed. When I made my debut for Wales against Scotland at Murrayfield in 1969 I remember receiving the ball on the halfway line and hearing Barry calling for it. I slung it to him and we ended up making 40 yards. He'd done all the hard work but somehow I was left with the feeling that it wouldn't have happened if I hadn't made the pass. The truth is, anyone playing club rugby could have passed him the ball.

"I remember being struck by their enthusiasm. They had the ability to make everyone around them better. That's the key to being a great player. There's no point being the best player in the world if you aren't going to get your teammates involved. They knew that. They realised very early on that no matter how good you are you're not going to win too many games on your own."

The 13-3 victory in the third test gave the Lions a 2-1 lead going into the final test of the series at Eden Park. The occasion took on even more importance when it was revealed this would be Meads' last test. There was a determination within the All Black camp to give him a memorable send-off by recording a win and levelling the series.

The stakes were just as high for the Lions. In four previous visits the Lions had failed each time. In 1930 they lost 3-1, in 1950 they lost the series 3-0 after drawing the first test in Dunedin, in 1959 they were sent home 3-1 losers and in the previous visit, in 1966, the All Blacks had scored 13 tries on their way to a 4-0 clean sweep.

As the '71 Lions bussed their way to Eden Park through the massive Auckland crowd, the tension was unbearable. Williams was as nervous as any of them. He knew the side was a game away from making history. Not knowing what to do with himself – his teammates were silent as they stared out of the windows – Williams stood up and made a declaration: "I'm going to drop a goal today!"

The bus erupted with laughter. Kicking was not a specialty of John Peter Rhys Williams. He'd managed only two dropped goals in his career until that day – one while playing for Bridgend against Bristol and the other for Wales against Fiji on the way home from the 1969 New Zealand tour. "I don't know why I said it," says Williams. "I think I just wanted to ease the tension a bit."

History records that it was Williams' drop goal midway through the second half that secured the series victory for the Lions. It didn't matter to Williams that when he took the kick he was 40 metres out from the posts. It didn't matter that he wasn't a specialist kicker. And it certainly didn't matter that the series was on the line. The kick was a mighty one – people who were there will tell you the ball was still rising when it sailed between the posts. It gave the Lions a 14-11 lead and while Mains was to reply with a 72nd-minute penalty, it was not enough to deny the Lions their series win.

"There's no question that kicking that goal was a defining moment for me. The ironic thing is that if we were going forward at the time I wouldn't have had a chance to kick it. As it was, the All Blacks were pushing us backwards. When I received the pass from David Duckham I didn't think I had any option but to kick. When it went through the posts I couldn't resist waving to the reserves in the stand as if to say 'I told you so!' At the time my teammates were as shocked as anyone else. I think some of them were convinced I was kicking for touch! They obviously knew what I knew – I was a fullback who didn't have much of a kicking game... that's why I always tried to run the ball."

Indeed, Williams' ability and wanting to run the ball at all costs was a feature of the tour. While the All Blacks were intent on 10-man rugby, the Lions' expansive game was a key to their 2-1 series win.

"As a back it was very exciting to win a test series even though we were getting only 40 percent of the ball. Because the All Black forwards were so strong, we knew we had to take chances when the ball came our way. The order from John was that any ball we got, we moved.

"I was fortunate that all the teams I played for played the sort of rugby which encouraged me to be an attacking fullback. I still believe that the fullback's number one job is in defence but once I'd taken care of things there, I'd always look to attack.

"I think I would have been bored stiff playing for the All Blacks of that era. For whatever reason, I always got the feeling that the All Black backs weren't being allowed to express themselves. They had some marvellously talented players but at times you wouldn't have known it. I doubt that if I'd been a New Zealander their selectors would have had a look at me. I'm sure they would have thought I was too adventurous.

"The same could probably be said for a lot of the Welsh backs of that time. There was something very special about playing for Wales in those days. Like all great teams, it was never enough for us simply to win. We had to win with style. We had to entertain. The coach used to give us his last-minute team talk then, as soon as he left the dressing-room, Gareth or Phil Bennett or someone like that would say 'Bullshit. Let's just enjoy ourselves.'

"We were spontaneous players and the good thing was that none of us were greedy. We all knew it would be someone else's turn to score the try which would win the game next time. We had eight or nine world-class players. We liked to express ourselves because that's the way we'd been brought up and Cardiff Arms Park was our canvas, if you like.

"Our upbringing was to enjoy the game. If you enjoy it, you play well; and if you play well, you win. There is a huge difference in ideals between going out on the field wanting to win in style, compared with not wanting to lose."

Williams didn't know it when he dropped that goal, but that day on Eden Park was to be the last time he'd experience victory against the All Blacks. The joy of being a part of a Lions' series victory in New Zealand still rates as the career highlight – better even than the Lions' series win in South Africa in 1974.

"It was a great achievement to win in the republic but, to be honest, we were never going to lose that series. I would much rather play in a tight test match than win one easily. Playing at the elite level, you want to be tested. There is no real joy in winning a series you should win as compared to being the underdogs and upsetting the champions. There was no World Cup in those days but I can't imagine winning the World Cup could match what we were feeling that day in Auckland."

One of Williams' fondest memories of that day at Eden Park came from an All Black lock. Meads, despite losing his one and only series as captain, was the first to congratulate the Lions on their victory. "He was a big man that day. He showed us all what character was about. He'd just played his last test, but there he was, congratulating us and wishing us well."

Ironically, remembering the end to the Cardiff test seven years later, it was another lock, Andy Haden, who would forever put a question mark around All Black "character" in the Welsh valleys.

❧

TWO decades have passed since Williams played the last of his 55 tests for Wales but he still looks the same as he did when he was the most feared fullback in rugby. The Sgt Pepper's Lonely Hearts Club Band hairstyle may be groomed and tinged with grey but it still worn longish, the mutton-chop sideburns have undergone but a token trim and the distinguishing scar on his right cheek, a bullet hole wound inflicted by a stray All Black stud, is a permanent reminder of more dangerous times – specifically, a reminder of one of the ugliest incidents in international rugby. If the goings-on at the Arms Park in 1978 weren't enough for the most ardent fan of sport and controversy, the ante was upped later on that All Black tour when, after completing the Grand Slam with test wins against Ireland, Wales, England and Scotland, the New Zealanders headed to Bridgend for a game to celebrate the club's centenary.

Williams' memories of the game are sketchy. He can remember the Bridgend team being fired up for the game. Wales' coach John Dawes had labelled the All Blacks "one of the most boring sides to tour Britain" but nothing could hide their record. The Bridgend game provided the Welsh with their last chance of glory. They were determined to join Swansea (1935), Cardiff (1953), Newport (1963) and Llanelli (1972) as Welsh clubs to defeat the All Blacks. From the start of the game it was obvious the passion of the Welsh and the dogged determination of the All Blacks to quell their enthusiasm was a recipe for an explosive game.

It wasn't long before trouble erupted. Williams found himself at the bottom of an All Black ruck with Canterbury prop John

Ashworth hovering over him. As Ashworth attempted to clear the ball his boot came into contact with Williams' face. One of Ashworth's sprigs had pierced Williams' right cheek and he left the field with blood pouring out of the open wound. Ashworth has long denied stomping on Williams but in his book *Mourie's All Blacks,* New Zealand's most respected rugby scribe, Sir Terry McLean, writes: "Ashworth moved each foot, or boot, in the time honoured motions of raking for the ball. The first movement might be forgiven. Williams' head was a long way from the ball. But in these early minutes the passion in the play was extreme; even a saint might have rushed, as Ashworth did, to win the ball for his team. The second movement was inexcusable. He rucked without due care and attention. Within the Road Code, driving without due care and attention can be a fatal fault. If Ashworth could not see any possible advantage could accrue to his team from his act, he was displaying an indiscipline out of character with the tour and the tenets of the game. Bridgend was his business. It was a bad business."

Williams has no doubt the act was deliberate and there is still bitterness about the incident. Surprisingly, the bitterness is not directed towards Ashworth. It's the All Black management team of the day – manager Russ Thomas and coach Jack Gleeson – who bear the brunt of Williams' displeasure.

"There's no doubt the incident at Bridgend was the saddest day in the history of games between Welsh sides and touring All Black teams," says Williams. "But I'm not bitter about the incident. I don't know why John Ashworth did what he did but there are a lot of rugby players who come to the end of their careers and look back at things they regretted doing on the rugby pitch. I don't hold any grudges against John. But what I am bitter about is that the All Black management pretended the incident never happened. The thing that really hurt me was when I was playing for the Barbarians against the New Zealanders the following week they brought John on as a replacement when Brad Johnstone couldn't continue. The fact the All Blacks did that, well, that hurt me more than being stomped on.

"It was obvious what had happened the week before and all the management had to do was to acknowledge the incident and stand John down for the last game of the tour. That's all they had to do. Instead, John came on as a replacement. It was a hurtful moment for me. It was an unfortunate way for the tour to end. Their management team had a lot to answer for in my opinion."

It says much for Williams that despite the disappointments of 1978 the respect he has for the black jersey is as strong as it was when he first watched film of the All Blacks' battles with the Lions as a 10-year-old during the 1959 tour.

"The respect is built out of years of trying to beat them and years of frustrations because we never did," he says. Williams' only test wins came in the Lions' jersey. In the Welsh strip, he ended his career with a no win/five loss record. Wales' best chance of victory looked like being in 1972 when their star-studded team hosted an All Black side that was definitely vulnerable. Ian Kirkpatrick's team had already suffered losses to Llanelli and the English North-Western Counties team. The All Black scrum was a weak point during the tour and the stuttering backline for the test included two new caps – fullback Joe Karam and winger Grant Batty. In contrast, the Welsh side featured names like Williams, Gerald Davies, John Bevan, Gareth Edwards, Mervyn Davies, John Taylor, Delme Thomas and Derek Quinnell, who had all toured New Zealand with the successful Lions' team in 1971.

A try by All Black prop Keith Murdoch set the All Blacks on their way to a 19-16 win.

"It was heartbreaking," says Williams. "The respect for the All Blacks comes from games like these because even though on paper we had a team that were perhaps slightly better, the All Blacks proved too difficult to beat. The All Blacks are always great competitors. They have an ability to frustrate their opponents. It was obvious the thrill of pulling on that black jersey means as much to a New Zealander as it does for a Welshman to pull on the Wales jersey. The All Blacks hadn't shown too many signs on that tour that they would be able to lift their game at the Arms Park. But they lifted their game all right."

Williams would play only one other test against New Zealand – the centenary test at Cardiff in 1980, when he was on the wrong side of a record 23-3 scoreline.

But it's those disappointments that make the memories of the Lions' victory in New Zealand nine years earlier so momentous.

"It's like anything in life; you remember the good things first. I don't think you can fully appreciate the good times unless you have been through the hard times... and there were plenty of those. But, to be honest, when I look back at the battles we lost against the All Blacks, there is something okay about the losses because we were beaten by the best competitors in the world. That's why any victory against them is so precious."

JPR WILLIAMS AGAINST THE ALL BLACKS

Date	For	Venue	Result	Score	Points
31-5-69	Wales	Christchurch	lost	0-19	
14-6-69	Wales	Auckland	lost	12-33	
26-6-71	British Isles	Dunedin	won	9-3	
10-7-71	British Isles	Christchurch	lost	12-22	
31-7-71	British Isles	Wellington	won	13-3	
14-8-71	British Isles	Auckland	drew	14-14	dg
2-12-72	Wales	Cardiff	lost	16-19	
27-1-73	Barbarians	Cardiff	won	23-11	
27-11-74	Welsh XV	Cardiff	lost	3-12	
11-11-78	Wales	Cardiff	lost	12-13	
13-12-78	Bridgend	Bridgend	lost	6-17	
1-11-80	Wales	Cardiff	lost	3-22	

TEST MATCH CAREER

	P	W	L	D	T	C	P	Dg	Pts
vs All Blacks	9	2	6	1	-	-	-	1	3
All Tests	63	43	14	6	6	2	3	1	39